Songs of Kabir
from the
Adi Granth

Songs of Kabir
from the
Adi Granth

Translation and Introduction by
Nirmal Dass

State University of New York Press

Cover Photo: Shows a supposed portrait of Kabir (Mughal, 17th century). Reproduced by the courtesy of the Oriental Antiquities Department, British Museum.

Published by
State University of New York Press, Albany

For information, address State University of New York Press,
State University Plaza, Albany, N.Y., 12246

Production by Marilyn Semerad
Marketing by Theresa A. Swierzowski

Library of Congress Cataloging-in-Publication Data

Kabir, 15th cent.
    [Poems. English. Selections]
    Songs of Kabir from the Adi Granth / translation and introduction
by Nirmal Dass.
        p. cm.
    ISBN 0-7914-0560-5. — ISBN 0-7914-0561-3 (pbk.)
    I. Dass, Nirmal, 1962-   . II. Title.
PK2095.K3A2326   1991
891'.4312—dc20   90-34852
                                                                          CIP

10 9 8 7 6 5 4 3 2 1

Parentibus meis
et
Danae

Contents

Preface

Texts canonized as scripture address an audience united by shared religious beliefs. Text and audience presume a common ground, namely, a transcendent reality or God, in whom truth is fully vested. But what happens to such texts in our post-Nietzschean world? What do we do with scriptures when most of us do not believe in their Author? For example, the ideological content of these songs of Kabir is generally to show that God is ultimate truth. Already we may not expect to respond to their primary purpose. Then why read them? Is there anything left in the scriptures of the world once belief is removed? On one level what remains is *scriptura*, which is liminal and errant; on another, we are left with texts that keep us unsure by raising questions that perpetually escape easy answers.

When Nietzsche announced the death of God, he also reminded us that this event, this message, is still on its way; it has still not reached most people. Perhaps these scriptures, these songs, are also still wandering; they force us to come to terms with the Nietzschean event, and keep us from taking the easy road of merely talking about recreating a past long vanished. We live between two kinds of death (God's and our own). All scriptures deny both. And yet some trace of the event perhaps remains which will reach our ears—for what we read is also what we hear.

I raise these questions not to answer them but because they ultimately became my *lex scripta* as I translated these songs. These songs/questions only lead us deeper into an ever-more complex labyrinth, which contains not a still, locatable center, but at its heart yet another maze. In this wandering journey, we are part of many texts, many books, many scriptures that we (as individuals and institutions) co-author. This text has no boundaries; it is and will be ever-Protean. Where Kabir signed once, "I" too sign and give my own authority, fully aware of my marginality and liminality — for my language here commands no "correct" or final meaning. In these songs, meanings are always transitional.

Introduction

I

The songs of Kabir translated here are part of Sikh scripture, and as such they hold a unique position in the Kabir canon. The Sikh community was founded in the fifteenth century, in the Panjab, by Guru Nanak. Consequently, these songs expound not only Kabir's own concepts, but also Sikh piety itself; they come down to us unchanged from at least 1604/5, when the fifth guru, Arjan Dev, codified all the songs of previous gurus and saints into one book, the *Adi Granth,* written in the Gurmukhi script.

Kabir's songs in this recension are in the eastern dialect of Hindi, with some admixture of Panjabi. They are filled with a particular freshness of image, style, and expression in their approach to the ancient problem of spirituality—for they question the very nature of spirituality and religiousity. This questioning speaks to our own age quite strongly, where distrust of systems is prevalent. We read these songs not for instruction or pleasure, but because they lead us to thinking; and the *telos* of thinking is not the arrival at an answer, but the provoking of thought which permits us to examine our role in all that exists. These songs set us on our way toward this examination.

The entire work of Kabir has come down to us in three major recensions: Eastern (the *Bijak*), Rajasthani (*Kabir Granthavali*), and from the Panjab (the *Adi Granth*). The first two have been thoroughly studied, edited, and translated, but the third has not really been dealt with on its own, although various translations and studies of the *Adi Granth* exist.[1]

These recensions differ from one another, but on the whole the Rajasthani recension has more hymns and *slokas* in common with the *Adi Granth*. Even a brief comparison with these other recensions permits us to ask the interesting question: Why were certain songs of Kabir chosen for inclusion in the *Adi Granth* and not others? Any attempt to answer this question necessarily leads us

1

into the very heart of Sikh piety, with its close link with medieval Northern Indian religious traditions.

It is only in recent times that standard editions of the *Bijak* and the *Kabir Granthavali* have been established.[2] The Panjab recension differs from these two in that it is pre-edited: It is part of an anthology (the *Adi Granth*[3]) of mystical songs by various *bhagats* ("Saints") and Sikh gurus, compiled by Guru Arjan Dev in 1604. This suggests that these songs have been carefully selected for their affirmation of Sikh doctrine; those that did not fit in were simply excluded. We can find evidence for this theologically manipulative editing in three forms. First of all we have the appending of verses by the editor, Guru Arjan Dev himself, but under the name of Kabir, to a song by Kabir (*Gauri,* 14). Secondly, there is the inclusion of whole poems by the editor into the *Songs of Kabir* (*Bhairo* 12; *Slokas* 209 – 211, 214, 221). Lastly, a *sloka* by the third Sikh guru, Amar Das, has been placed among Kabir's *Slokas* (no. 220). These examples are in fact instances of affirmation of Kabir's work: There is agreement, endorsement, and, if need be, clarification. The question that naturally arises is, why not leave these instances out? Their importance lies in the fact that Sikh tradition does not differentiate between Kabir's own work and the emendations, additions, and interpolations by the two gurus. A particular sense of authorship is at play here. The Sikh gurus all took the pseudonym "Nanak," the personal name of their first guru; this was to demonstrate continuity — the "spirit" of Nanak was embodied in all of them. The signature "Nanak" authorized a poetic utterance. When Guru Arjan Dev and Guru Amar Das approach Kabir's work, they freely move within it also in order to highlight this continuity — what Kabir said is what the two gurus say — the tradition, the utterance, begun by Kabir is now being completed.

Since these translations are not only of Kabir's songs, but also about the songs of Kabir within Sikh piety, I have chosen to retain these interpolations and additions as they have come down to us in the *Adi Granth.* But in order to fully realize the nature of this affirmation, let us briefly indicate the context of Kabir's own doctrinal position.[4]

It has long been recognized that Kabir is to be understood within the *sant* ("mendicant") tradition of northern India.[5] Of course, we must first of all clarify this tradition, since the *sants* were never a unified group. Indian religious sentiment has always harbored two attitudes: One that cherishes the Vedas and the Upanishads as the only true sources of spiritual and divine wisdom, and the other that firmly denies this scriptural authority in favor of enlightenment gained through personal experience of the Supreme. The Buddha is the best example of the latter; and it is in that tradition that we can locate the *sants*. Thus tradition should not be understood as received precepts and authority, but rather as an attitude that seeks to either accept or deny religious systematization.

On the whole, the *sants* sought to deny the accepted notions of the holy — they rejected the Vedas, the Upanishads, idol-worship, ritual, Brahminism, and hence also the caste system; in brief, they denied external, visible manifestations themselves. What they advocated was internal — inexpressible, unworded inner love and devotion (*bhakti*) for a Godhead that was itself internal, non-incarnated, without attributes (*nirgun*). The divine was blended in all of creation; it was the primal essence diluted in all things.

The loving devotee could fathom the unfathomable only by realizing this presence: The divine was as close as oneself — *esse est deus*. In effect, devotion was to be centered upon the God beyond God, whose abode was silence, who was not the many, perhaps in the same sense as Neoplatonic henological metaphysics, which defined God as the ground of all things. *Bhakti* meant meditating upon the "Name" (*nam*) and not the form (*rupa*), at first aided by a human guru (himself already merged with God), later by oneself. The Name itself freed one from all names and led one to the Supreme; it was the *nomen omninominabile et nomen innominabile* that Meister Eckhart struggled with. Salvation required breaking the cycle of transmigration to gather the separate fragment of the divine back into the Godhead, when the individual soul itself became part of God. And it was love and devotion alone which united the two, like long-expectant lovers. But if this opportunity for union was neglected and missed, then the individual again wandered, never complete — like lovers never to be united.

The role of the guru in this process of salvation must be underscored. For Kabir, as for the *sants* in general, the guru was the immediate representation of the divine, one who had already arrived at the perfected state, and who helped others achieve that state of perfection; this is a concept quite close to the Buddhist notion of the *boddhisatva*. The guru's instruction (*shabad*), frequently called "grace," produced illumination, which awoke the sleeping soul into an awareness of the divine. The *shabad* was part of the divine since it led the soul to unite with the Supreme (like the Johannine principle of *logos*); given this revelatory power, the *shabad* effectively negated all other methods (largely scriptural) of enlightenment. The *shabad* awoke the soul to the internal divine, the state of truth, which brought about an experience beyond communication: The individual soul, the *shabad*, and the divine merged and blended into one.

Given their denial of scripture, tradition, and ritual, the majority of the *sants* were from the lower castes, and their medium was the vernacular commonly spoken (*bhasha*), unlike Sanskrit, which was strictly controlled by Brahmins and understood by a mere handful. Thus their message had a wider reception; and this appeal was heightened by the fact that the medium was poetry, easily memorized, easily sung. They advocated the responsibilities of house and work (*grihasti*), rather than renunciation of the world (*sanyas*). As a result the *sants* did not abandon their traditional tasks: Ravidas remained a cobbler, Sain a barber, Kabir a weaver, Namdev a calico-printer.

One other influence discernible in the *sant* doctrine is Nathism. The *naths* were yogis who followed the teachings of Gorakh Datta (ca. 12th century), who advocated salvation through yoga and asceticism, combined with tantric and Buddhist elements.[6] They practised *hatha-yoga,* in order to physically experience the mystical union between God and the individual. Again, this led to an internalizing doctrine: External manifestations such as temples, rituals, scriptures, idols, and the caste system were rigidly denied. Once the individual underwent this experience, he (Nathism is largely misogynist) became a spiritual adept, a human-god. Important also is the fact that the *naths* spread their message by way of the vernacular, rather than Sanskrit.[7]

It is within this context that Kabir's songs have their being.[8] Thus, even though Kabir disagreed with yogic practice as such, and any form of *avatar*-worship in the *saguni* tradition, that is, God manifesting himself throughout time, he nevertheless drew greatly upon the attitudes engendered by *sants* and *naths*. He stressed the need for internal, unmediated love and adoration turned toward the *nirguni* divine, which led to the end of the cycle of rebirth and brought about union with the Supreme. This doctrine merged directly with Sikh piety, and as a result Kabir's place in the *Adi Granth* became secure. Those hymns that suggested the divinity of Kabir the man, as in the ones in the *Kabirpanthi* tradition, were excluded, and those that needed explanation were clarified by way of editorial intervention.

The works of Kabir in the *Adi Granth* are part of an anthology of mystical songs by the Sikh gurus and Hindu and Muslim saints (*bhagats* and Sufis). It is interesting to trace the evolution of the *Adi Granth* as scripture, closely tied as it is to the development of the Sikh faith itself.

Sikhism is generally seen as having gone through three stages, each one embodying a particular characteristic of the faith.[9] For convenience, these stages can be associated with three of the ten gurus, namely, Guru Nanak (1469–1539), Guru Arjan Dev (1563–1606), and Guru Gobind Singh (1666–1708).[10] Guru Nanak established the new faith doctrinally, structurally, and scripturally. Certainly, these underwent changes at the hands of each of the subsequent gurus; however, the foundations can be attributed to Guru Nanak. Doctrinally, he clarified and summarized the vast theology of the *sants*. Structurally, he established the *sangat* ("congregation"), which met regularly to sing hymns and to meditate, the *dharamsala* ("religious hall"), which provided a place for worship, and the *pangat* (also known as the *langar*, the communal kitchen) attached to the *dharamsala*, which served to physically break all barriers between caste. Scripturally, he negated the importance of the Hindu holy books, and in their place established hymns of his own, and perhaps of other *bhagats* and Sufis.

The second stage is a pivotal one, since it markedly changed Sikhism. Guru Arjan's reign led to two things: the compilation of the *Adi Granth*, and the subsequent militarization of the Sikh community. In 1604, he compiled and edited an anthology of mystical poetry that became the holy book of the Sikhs, and with great reverence installed it in the Harimandir (the Golden Temple) in Amritsar. This early veneration of the written word of the gurus, *bhagats*, and Sufis perhaps can be associated with Guru Gobind Singh's later declaration of the holy book as guru. Important also is the fact that the *Adi Granth* firmly established Sikhism as a religion, rather than a sect of Hinduism, and it clearly distinguished the Sikhs as a community. Arjan was also the first of the gurus to have been born a Sikh (the previous four had been born Hindus and had converted to Sikhism). He created the *daswandh* (tithe) tax, which gave him enough revenues to construct various buildings and water reservoirs; the most famous of these buildings was the Golden Temple, whose construction began in 1589.

He was also the first Sikh martyr. All his life he was challenged by his older brother, Prithi Chand, who wanted to be guru. Legend has it that Prithi Chand was a personal friend of the Muslim Moghul emperor Jahangir, whom he turned against Arjan. Eventually Guru Arjan was tortured and killed by the order of Jahangir because he had helped prince Khusrau, Jahangir's son, who had been nominated as emperor by the Emperor Akbar, Jahangir's father, during the prince's flight from Jahangir.[11] Guru Arjan's murder entirely changed the previously peaceful Sikh community into an aggressively militarized one. His son, Guru Har Gobind, who succeeded him, dedicated himself to this task: He kept soldiers as retainers, he erected the *Akal Takht*, where he sat in state like a king rather than a guru, and he built a fort, Lohgarh, in Amritsar.[12]

The last stage comes with the creation of the Khalsa, a society of warrior-saints, whose ideals were to defend the weak and the innocent, fight injustice and oppression, and uphold truth and righteousness, with the sword if need be. This militarization was the result of Muslim persecution and attempts at suppression of the Sikhs. Tradition has it that during the Baisakhi (spring) festival of 1699, Guru Gobind Singh founded the Khalsa order, where he thoroughly melded together Sikh theology and a martial outlook. Important also is the fact that he brought the line of gurus to an end by not appointing a successor (his own four sons were killed in his lifetime), proclaiming the *Adi Granth* itself as the manifest guru.

But let us return again to the second stage in the development of Sikhism, in order to look at the history and nature of the *Adi Granth*. In 1603–1604, Guru Arjan had a tank dug in Amritsar, naming it Ramsar ("The Pool of God"), and beside it compiled the holy book. Although these actions seem spontaneous, it is more than likely that the compilation was a political act. Since

Arjan's father, Guru Ram Das, had passed over his two older sons in favor of Arjan, there had been continual problems for Guru Arjan, largely created by his elder brother, Prithi Chand, already mentioned. One of these challenges was the writing of verses under the name of "Nanak" by Prithi Chand and his son Manohar Dass Meharban (Nanak was the name assumed by each spiritual leader of the Sikhs on becoming guru, which became also his pen-name). In the face of these counterfeit verses, Guru Arjan's decision must be seen as an attempt to control and ultimately discredit such compositions by codifying the true verses of the gurus in an authorized version.

His effort, however, was not the first in Sikhism, for an earlier collection, put together by Guru Amar Das and copied by his grandson Sahans Ram, existed in two volumes. This is commonly known as the Goindwal *pothis* (books). These *pothis* were in the possession of Baba Mohan, the son of Guru Amar Das, and consisted of the works of the first three gurus and the songs of Kabir, Namdev, Trilochan, Sain, Ravidas, and Jaidev.[13] Thus placing the works of the gurus alongside those of the *sants* can be traced as far back as the Mohan *pothis,* if not earlier, and Guru Arjan incorporated these into his own *Granth.*

In addition to the verses of the first four gurus, he also included his own work, and those of other *bhagats* and Sufis. He also expunged some poems of the saints and clarified many others, as already shown. He arranged the poems according to musical settings (*ragas*), in order to inculcate certain moods expressed by the songs themselves.[14] Later on, the tenth guru, Gobind Singh, added the songs of his father, Guru Tegh Bahadur, to the *Adi Granth;* he did not include his own work in the *Adi Granth.*[15] Thus, only six of the first nine gurus composed verses.

The completed version came to about six thousand hymns. The distribution of authorship by the gurus themselves is as follows: Guru Nanak (974), Guru Angad (62), Guru Amar Das (907), Guru Ram Das (679), Guru Arjan Dev (2,218), and Guru Tegh Bahadur (115). The contributions of *bhagats* and Sufis are: Jaidev (2), Farid (134), Beni (3), Namdev (60), Trilochan (4), Parmanand (1), Sadhana (1), Ramananda (1), Dhanna (4), Pipa (1), Sain (1), Kabir (541), Ravidas (41), Bhikan (2), and Sur Das (2).[16] Included also are various odes by court poets and musicians employed by the gurus.

Structurally, the *Adi Granth* falls into three sections: Introductory (containing hymns that have acquired liturgical importance and use); the *Ragas* (containing the hymns of six gurus followed by those of the saints), in all 31; then a miscellany of works that did not quite fit the previous two categories. It is in this section that we find the *Slokas* of Kabir and also those of the Sufi, Farid.

It is often said that the *Adi Granth* recension of Kabir's songs is the oldest, since it was definitely in existence by 1603–1604.[17] It has already been noted that Guru Arjan based his anthology upon the Mohan *pothis,* compiled by Guru Amar Das. We have no records of how the verses of the first two gurus were preserved and handed down; perhaps Guru Amar Das inherited the works upon his ascension to guruship. But we do know that the Mohan *pothis* included the works of various *bhagats*. There are, however, textual indications that suggest that Guru Nanak himself was acquainted with the Kabir corpus that would later appear in the *Adi Granth*. Intertextuality is at play here, where we can see the songs of Kabir setting the stage for the verses of Guru Nanak. It is worthwhile to trace this intertextual play within the songs of Guru Nanak and Kabir.

In song number 24, in *Raga Asa,* Kabir says:

My body is a dye-tub:
I will dye my heart with purity.
The five virtues
will be my wedding guests,
and I will walk
around the fire with Ram Rai,
my soul suffused with His color.

Sing, sing, O maidens, songs of marriage:
Ram, my husband, has come to my house. (Rest)

In the lotus of my breath
I have planted the marriage canopy;
divine wisdom
is my marriage mantra.
Ram Rai has become
my husband:
Great has been my luck.

Wise men, saints, and ascetics
came to my marriage
in three million
three hundred thousand chariots.
Kabir says, "The one divine Bhagwan
has taken me away in marriage."

Let us juxtapose to this a song by Guru Nanak, also in *Raga Asa,*
number 10:

Showing mercy, He came to my house;
my friends got together and arranged things.
Seeing this bustle, my heart filled with joy:
the Bridegroom has come to wed me.

Sing, sing, O maidens, songs of marriage:
Jagjivan, my husband, has come to my house. (Rest)

My marriage took place at the guru's door;
I knew my husband the moment I met Him.
His Word pervades the whole world;
my heart exulted and I lost my pride.

He looks after His own affairs;
He does not depend upon others.
These affairs are truth, contentment, mercy, faith;
only a few pious ones guess this.

Nanak declares, "The Husband of all
is He alone. She upon whom
He looks with grace
is the blissful bride."

(As an aside, the literary convention of the poet addressing him/
herself by name should be clarified. The practice is commonly
found in northern Indian poetry of this period. It is known as
bhanita or *takhallus* and serves as a signature. On the level of discourse we have the interesting combination of the poem itself and
the poet as the addressee). Beside the fact that both songs are in
the same *raga,* we find that the stanzas with a rest exactly parallel
each other. Also, Guru Nanak's hymn seems intent on elaborating

and expanding the subtleties present in Kabir's verses, such as how the marriage took place, who arranged it, and the definition of a happy bride. In another song in *Raga Asa* (no. 30), Kabir says:

> I adorned myself for our tryst,
> but Hari, Jagjivan, Gosain never came.
>
> Hari is my husband;
> I am Hari's bride.
> Ram is great,
> and I am a frail girl. (Rest)
>
> Wife and husband live in one house;
> they share one bed — but there is no union.
>
> Blessed is the bride who pleases her Beloved.
> Kabir, say, "She will not suffer rebirth."

Again, Guru Nanak expands on what is hinted at in Kabir in two songs in *Raga Asa* (nos. 26 and 27):

> I have not one virtue with which to cleanse myself;
> my Husband lies awake and I sleep fitfully.
>
> This will not endear me to my Spouse;
> my Husband lies awake and I sleep fitfully. (Rest)
>
> Though I come filled with desire to His bed,
> I cannot know if I please Him or not.
>
> I know not what will happen, O my mother;
> I cannot live without beholding my Lord. (Rest)
>
> I never tasted love; my thirst was never quenched.
> Now my youth has fled and I am filled with regret.
>
> I still lie awake thirsting with desire;
> I am saddened and without hope. (Rest)
>
> If a woman adorn herself with pride's loss,
> then will she stay in her Husband's bed.

Then, Nanak, will she please her Master's heart;
giving up pride, she will unite with her Lord.

In song number 27, we read:

In her parents' house, the woman stands like a child:
I know not the true worth of my Husband.

My Husband is one, and none other;
by His grace we may meet. (Rest)

At her in-laws, the woman realizes the truth,
and easily, calmly recognizes her Beloved.

By the guru's grace she can obtain wisdom
with which she can please her Husband.

Nanak says, "If she adorn herself with love,
she will ever adorn her Lord's bed."

It is the plight of Kabir's "frail girl" that Guru Nanak is expanding, explicating how to please the Beloved and attain gratification.
    There are various other examples of intertextuality. For example, Kabir's song number 25, in *Raga Asa* (pp. 141 – 142) should be read with Guru Nanak's hymn in *Raga Asa*, number 22:

The body is an unfired pot,
suffering birth and death.
How can we cross this horrid world-ocean;
it is impossible without the guru Hari.

There is no one else but You, my Beloved;
there is no one else but You, O Hari.
In all colors and shapes are You;
You forgive those on whom You look with grace. (Rest)

My horrid mother-in-law won't let me stay home
nor let me meet my Beloved.
Since I fell at the feet of my friends,
the guru Hari turned to me in grace.

By knowing and stifling my heart, I realized
there is no friend like You.
I stay where You put me,
enduring pain and solace as You see fit.

I have forsaken both hopes and wishes,
disappointed by the three virtues.
The pious ones obtain the fourth stage,
taking protection in the company of saints.

Wisdom, meditation, all worship and penance
will be theirs in whose hearts is the Invisible,
the Unknowable. Nanak, the heart dyed in Ram's name
will acquire calm devotion, under the guru's guidance.

Here Guru Nanak expands the trope, "horrid mother-in-law,"
into a lengthy description on ways to escape all the "in-laws" and
meet the Beloved.

Furthermore, there is an indication that one of Kabir's songs
(*Shri Raga,* no. 1) may already have been closely associated with a
hymn by Guru Nanak before the *Adi Granth* was compiled. Before
beginning the section on the verses of the various *bhagats* in *Shri
Raga,* Guru Arjan gives the following direction for singing the
first song, which is by Kabir. The Panjabi text reads: "Shri rag Kabir jio ka ek swan kai ghar gavna" ("Shri raga; [a song by] Kabir
to be sung in the same mode as "Ek Swan"). "Ek swan" are the first
two words of a song by Guru Nanak, also in *Shri Raga:*

One dog and two bitches are with me;
they bark at the wind each morning.
Filth is my dagger, carrion its handle.
I am like a hunter, O Creator.

I have neither honor nor good deeds;
my face is deformed and my appearance ugly.
Your one name saves the world—
that is my support, that is my nourishment. (Rest)

My mouth curses day and night;
I covet another's house; I am vile and base.

The untouchables, Wrath and Lust, live in my body.
I am like a hunter, O Creator.

Seeking to strangle, I dress like a saint;
I am a thug, in a land of thugs.
Though I see myself as clever, I am loaded down.
I am like a hunter, O Creator.

Being corrupt, I did not know Your works;
how can I show my face, being a wretch and a thief?
Base Nanak speaks these thoughts:
"I am like a hunter, O Creator."

This hymn makes manifest the "worldly pleasures, / which harbor
certain death" in Kabir's song. There must have been a tradition
that conflated the two songs in performance, indicating a link already established before the *Adi Granth.* There are various other
hymns which also demonstrate the play of intertextuality. For example, Guru Nanak's song number 38 in *Raga Asa* is closely
linked with Kabir's hymn number 1 in *Raga Ramkali;* Kabir's
Raga Ramkali 4 is connected with Guru Nanak's *Raga Ramkali* 1;
Kabir's *Raga Ramkali* 10 parallels Guru Nanak's *Raga Ramkali* 10.
Kabir's phrase "man jite jag jiteia" ("By conquering the heart, you
conquer the world," *Raga Maru,* no. 2) is repeated by Guru Nanak
in his *Japji* ("man jite jag jit," *Pauri* 28). Similar phrases occur in
Kabir's *Raga Basant,* 3, in Guru Nanak's *Raga Asa* 2, in Kabir's
Raga Sarang 2, and in Guru Nanak's *Raga Ramkali* 9. These various interpenetrations of the two texts suggest that one of the texts
(Guru Nanak's) assumes the pre-existence of another (Kabir's).
Thus we can assume that the collection of Kabir's verses later to
be anthologized in the *Adi Granth* was in Guru Nanak's possession. There is also textual evidence that this collection probably
was passed on to Guru Amar Das, whose hymns also show this in-
terpenetration.

In this translation, the order given to Kabir's hymns in the
Adi Granth is maintained. Each song appears under a particular
raga, i.e., the mode in which it is to be sung. Since a *raga* is a fluid
musical structure, it can be combined with another. Hence, one
gets combinations such as Gauri-Cheti, Gauri-Bairagan, Gauri-
Purabi, and Basant-Hindola. Basically, these are instructions for
singers as to the kind of musical measure most suited to the words.

II

Of Kabir the man, very little is known. We are still no further in ascertaining the particulars of Kabir's biography than was Ahmad Shah, when he declared some seventy years ago that "two facts only can be asserted with absolute confidence: he [Kabir] lived for some time at Kashi [Kanshi] (Benares), and he died at Maghar [Magahar]."[18] The whole issue of Kabir's life is hotly contested; what we possess can best be described as mythical and largely hagiographical.[19] The works that deal with some aspects of the life of Kabir are works of Indian hagiography, *Kabir-panthi* writings, the verses of various *sants,* and historical works. However, none of these place Kabir in any definable historical context; most extol his greatness, his spiritual strength, and his supernatural abilities. The contribution of these works is best summed up by Vaudeville, when she states that, "The most ancient and reliable testimonies, as we have seen, do not throw any light on Kabir's life; they rather stress his extraordinary personality and express a certain amount of perplexity about his teachings."[20]

But perhaps the shortcoming is ours rather than the tradition's, for the Indian perspective tends not to bifurcate the past into two parts, namely, one "historical" and the other legendary. The two merge, so that what we would call objective fact is inextricably interwoven with the legendary—is not factuality (history) itself a narrative (story), which adjusts itself to the socio-ideological paradigms of each generation, thereby engendering and ensuring change? Consequently, we must combine the historical and the hagiographical to study them as one in order to begin arriving at an understanding of Kabir. The signature "Kabir" in these songs is neither purely historical nor purely hagiographical; it is both together, existing always in the middle of the two, creating a third category of ascription. This third category is marked by inadequacy (what we know is never enough) and yet necessity (we must proceed with what we do know).

As soon as we begin historicizing Kabir, we touch off controversy. A simple matter like Kabir's dates immediately involves us in legend. Traditionally, he is supposed to have lived 120 years (1398–1518). As often pointed out, this lengthy lifespan permits him to be associated with other famous religious and historical personages such as Guru Nanak and Sikander Lodi, although no

link in fact can be established. The date of birth is strictly traditional. The year of death differs in verses that may have been
composed to record the passing of the saint:[21]

In the *Vikrami* year 1505 he went to Magahar.
In the light half of the moon, in the month of Agahan,
breath blended with breath.[22]

*   *   *   *   *

In the *Vikrami* year 1575 he went to Magahar.
In the light half of the moon, in the month of Magh,
breath blended with breath.[23]

The consensus on the whole favors the year given in the first version (1505, A.D. 1448),[24] since there is a memorial at Magahar
erected by Nawab Bijli Khan some time in 1450; the monument
was later repaired by Nawab Fidai Khan around 1567.[25] On the
other hand, devotees of Kabir favor the second version, since it
easily links him with Guru Nanak and Sikander Lodi.

Tradition claims that Kabir was the disciple of the Vaishnava
reformer, Ramananda (ca. fourteenth century), whose thought
affected mystical concepts in northern India. Ramananda was a
disciple of the great reformer Ramanuja and extended the message of *bhakti* (see Glossary) to the lower classes, which had been
largely excluded. Hence, tradition tells us that among his disciples
were the cobbler Ravidas, the butcher Dhanna, the barber Sain,
and the weaver Kabir; his other famous disciple is Tulsi Das. Ramananda eliminated the need for ritualized worship; true worship was opening oneself to the reality of Brahman, under the
guidance of a human guru.

If we seek certainty about Kabir the man, then we must turn
to the songs themselves (a work of faith in its own right, since the
assumption is that the text largely represents words actually uttered by Kabir the man). From these we learn that Kabir was a
weaver (*julaha*) by caste (*Gauri* 54, *Ramkali* 5, *Asa* 26, *Slokas* 2, 82).
And there is also the fact that he was a Muslim, although perhaps
only nominally, as indicated by his name ("Kabir" is one of the
ninety-nine mystical appellations of God in the Koran, meaning
"great"). These two facts would place Kabir at the lower end of the
Indian caste system, since he would be both low-born and a
mlechha ("infidel").

It is noteworthy that *julaha* is a Muslim term for a weaver; the Hindu designation is *kori*—Kabir uses both terms to refer to himself (*Asa* 36). This is perfectly in keeping with his rhetoric of continually placing himself outside the two religions. But on the whole, the Muslim element is rather small in these songs, which has led to studies of the religious tendencies of the (*julahas*) weavers.[26] The general consensus is that the weavers became Muslim for convenience but retained their own beliefs, a melange of Hinduism, Sufism, low Buddhism, and the tantric teachings of the *Naths*. It is these religious traditions that provide the foreground for the songs of Kabir, to which we shall now turn. In all this, as is fitting, the historical Kabir, the signatory of these songs, vanishes; the trace, the signature alone survives: "Kabir vanished when he shouted 'Ram' " (*Bhairo* 5).

Vaudeville (1974), after thoroughly expounding the context of Kabir's work, concludes:

> Death, its inescapable, frightful, tragic character, appears to be at the core of Kabir's thought. He speaks about it in the most vivid and blunt manner, using a variety of images and symbols mostly borrowed from popular tradition and direct, matter-of-fact observation. For him, as for the Tantrikas, Death—whether it be called Mic (*mrtyu*), Yamraj (*Yama-raja*), or Kal (*kala*) — remains the ultimate Enemy of all created beings, the insatiable Monster who has never been defeated . . . (147–148).

This observation, although perhaps true in itself, is ultimately not apt for the *Adi Granth* recension of Kabir's work. First of all, it is far too general—for in the final analysis death alone is the guarantor (in Jacques Derrida's sense) of all religious systems, and thus in no way peculiar to Tantric thought or to Kabir. More specifically, this remark obscures the role of Maya and devotion (love)—concepts which occur far more frequently than death in Kabir's songs. Death, within the rhetoric of these songs, is an illusion, part of Maya, which can be dispelled; it is a trope which underscores the divine ("reality"): God is beyond death.

And God himself is always portrayed as a lover. Thus what we arrive at is the game of love. If death is at the core of Kabir's songs, then death is most certainly decentred and peripheralized by love (*Shri Raga* 1; *Raga Gauri* 11, 12, 17, 18, 20, 32, 35, 46, 52, 55, 56, etc.):

> Kabir,
> the suttee climbs
> on to the pyre:
> "O cremation-ground,
> you are now my friend.
> Listen:
> You are all I have left—
> it is now
> I need you most" (*Sloka* 85).

Here, it is fire that will burn away all illusion (life, the body, and death), leaving reality (the soul, the divine), which is unseen but which alone can unite and blend with God by way of love—for the ideal suttee burns for love of her husband.

Love itself is a game (*lila*) played unendingly between God and the individual devotee; it encompasses all mystical experience (*parcha*) contained in these songs; and part of this game is death:

> O heart,
> put away doubt
> and dance fearlessly:
> All this is Maya's artifice.
> Does a bold warrior fear the battlefield?
> Does a suttee worry about pots and pans?
>
> Quit faltering,
> O my foolish heart:
> The vermilion-filled coconut
> is in your hand—
> now you must burn and receive renown (*Gauri* 68).

>   *   *   *   *   *

> Kabir,
> if you want to play
> the game of love,

then cut off your head
and use it as a ball.
You will be so carried away
with this game
that you won't know what
is taking place (*Sloka* 239).

*   *   *   *   *

Kabir,
if you want to play
the game of love,
play with a professional:
Crushing unripe mustard seeds
yields neither
oil-cakes nor oil (*Sloka* 240).

In the foreground of death, then, is always love and the game
of love. And this game has a plethora of different actions, activi-
ties, and functions. It involves the absence of the Beloved, the
soul's desire for the presence of this absent one, utterance of sorrow, visions of union, pining, enlightening fellow human beings,
singing praise, bliss, rapture, and death (destruction of the self
and the emergence of the divine). All these elements of the love-
game share equal importance in that each of them predetermines
the other in an unending chain of significances; thus to emphasize
one element (death, for instance) is to negate the others which sur-
round it. These songs of Kabir are not merely centered upon one
thing (e.g. death); their concern is with the interplay of the many
within the one: "From the same clay / the Shaper / shaped many
things" (*Parbhati*, 3).

The larger concern of these songs is to deal with the inability
of language to encompass all of experience. Again and again this
is brought home to us: "Kabir, say, 'It's like a mute eating sugar—
/ ask him and what can he say?' " (*Gauri* 51). The *Acrostic* also is
an attempt at enfolding within language the divine (that which is
alien to language) in order for semantics, and thought itself, to
proceed. But there is the immediate realization that although the
step into language is necessary, it is at the same time inadequate:

The three worlds are in these fifty-two letters:
All things are in them.

These letters will pass away—
but the letter for Him is not among these.

       *   *   *   *   *

Where there are words, you need letters;
where there are no words, the mind ceases to be.
He is present with or without words:
None can describe His reality.

       *   *   *   *   *

If I find the Unfindable, what will I say?
And if I do speak—to what end?
As the banyan tree is blended with the seed,
so He pervades the three worlds (*The Acrostic* 1, 2, 3).

We are again in the realm of language-games,[27] where God provides riddles and the human subject must guess them:

Only they can guess to whom He gives the riddle:
how can we live without guessing? (*Gauri* 51)

       *   *   *   *   *

Kabir says,
"The servant has found Him out—
I have solved the riddle,
by the guru's grace" (*Asa* 3).

       *   *   *   *   *

Kabir says, "Those who want to solve the riddle
will know all if they repeat 'Ram' " (*Asa* 22).

The riddles of the divine are expressed by the rhetorical device commonly known as the *ultvansi* (or *sandhyabhasha*).[28] Literally, *ultvansi* means "inverse language," while *sandhyabhasha* means "evening language." There has been much discussion as to the implications of the *ultvansi* songs,[29] but what has emerged is not really helpful, since we get such conclusions as, "Upside-down language *should* make you feel like a fool: that is part of its function."[30] Hess and Singh attempt to redefine the term *ultvansi* itself, but eventually end up reaffirming the previous understanding: "In most cases, 'upside-down' remains the most convenient translation."[31]

This reading, however, is paradigmatic of the *ultvansi* songs themselves: they are disruptive units within ordinary discourse which force us either to rethink language or fall back on surer ground (as proposed by Hess and Singh). All the various attempts at recovering and domesticating them fail, because they, like the divine, are alien to language, in that they exist outside the axioms of syntax and semantics. They are not made to make us feel like fools; rather they underscore the Upanishadic exclamation, *neti, neti* ("not this, not this"). Hence the discourse is beyond foolishness and understanding; these songs perpetually slip beyond linguistic grasp into an unnamed realm, like the divine, both present and absent at the same time: "Raja Ram, *akk*-pods [see note 6, p. 320] become ripe mangoes — / few can solve the riddle and eat them" (*Asa* 6). We are involved in a process of un-knowing the unknown through a *docta ignoranta;* the *ultvansi* songs demonstrate that which is not manifest: the hidden divine who vanishes behind his/its/her creation (we are very close to negative theology). These riddles disengage themselves from predicated existence within language, so that they may all the more affirm the superessentiality of God the unraveller: Kabir says, "Those who want to solve the riddle / will know all if they repeat 'Ram' " (*Asa* 22). Echoing in the distance is Meister Eckhart's prayer: "Therefore I pray God that he may make me free of God."[32]

III

Translation is arriving at a third text; for although it stems from the source text, it is not a part of it, and the translated text is not part of the target context, e.g., Kabir in English is a contradiction. As a result, the translated version exists on its own, becoming alien from both the source text and the target language. This is precisely Kabir's position; over and over again he says that he is neither Hindu nor Muslim—but a third unnamed name. In tracing Kabir in the *Adi Granth*,[33] scattered as he is in various sections and subsections, one realizes that the process is one of gathering fragments, which will never converge into a whole, but which will keep on breaking apart as one collects them. The *Rig Veda*, which is filled with *ultvansi* hymns, perhaps provides a clue as to why fragments perpetually break off:

Speech was split into four parts,
known by the inspired priests.
Three parts are hidden far away,
which people do not use.
It is the fourth part of speech
which is spoken by men.[34]

Walter Benjamin supplements this verse by stating that

a translation, instead of resembling the meaning of the original, must lovingly and in detail incorporate the original's
mode of signification, thus making both the original and the
translation recognizable as fragments of a greater language,
just as fragments are part of a vessel.[35]

The "greater language" is the "three parts hidden far away," re-
flected in Kabir's *ultvansi* songs and his refusal to be named a
Hindu or a Muslim: "One tree / yet countless shoots and
branches" (*Ramkali* 6).

Notes to Introduction

1. The translations of the *Bijak* are *A Translation of Kabir's Complete Bijak into English,* trans. Prem Chand (Calcutta: Baptist Mission, 1911); *The Bijak of Kabir,* trans. Ahmad Shah (1917; rpt. New Delhi: Asian Publication Services, 1977); and *The Bijak of Kabir,* trans. Linda Hess and Shukdev Singh (San Francisco: North Point Press, 1983). The *Kabir Granthavali* has been translated by Charlotte Vaudeville, *Kabir* (Oxford: Clarendon Press, 1974). The *Adi Granth* itself has also had translators, namely, E. Trumpp, *The Adi-Granth* (1877; rpt. New Delhi: Munshiram Manoharlal, 1970); M. A. Macauliffe, *The Sikh Religion* (1909; repr. New Delhi: S. Chand & Company, 1983); Manmohan Singh, *Shri Guru Granth Sahib* (Amritsar: Shromani Gurdwara Parbandhak Committee, 1962 – 1969); Gopal Singh, *Shri Guru Granth Sahib* (Delhi: Gurdas Kapur & Sons, 1962).

2. Vaudeville (1974) gives an extensive history of the various editions of the *Bijak* and the *Kabir Granthavali.* See her "Bibliography," pp. 333 – 336.

3. *Adi* means "first" and *granth* means "book." This differentiates it from the *granth* of the tenth Guru, Gobind Singh, the *Dasam Granth.* *Adi* refers to God, as well, so the title can also mean something like "Godbook."

4. See also Karine Schomer, "Kabir in the *Guru Granth Sahib:* An Exploratory Essay," in *Sikh Studies: Comparative Perspectives on a Changing Tradition,* ed. Mark Juergensmeyer and N. Gerald Barrier (Berkeley, Calif.: Berkeley Graduate Theological Union Religious Studies Series, 1979), pp. 75 – 86. She posits that the hymns of Kabir in the *Adi Granth* valorize social order and the role of the householder, and lack the misogynist tinge in other recensions.

5. See for example, the discussions in W. H. McLeod, *Guru Nanak and the Sikh Religion* (Oxford: Clarendon Press, 1968), and Vaudeville (1974).

6. Vaudeville (1974), pp. 81 ff, gives an important summary of Nathism.

7. The vernacular I am referring to is *sadhukhari* (also known as *santbhasha,* or *sadhuboli*). It was the *lingua franca* for the devotional writings, sayings, and songs of the *sants* in Northern India. Based upon *khari*

boli (Hindi spoken around Delhi), it drew from various other dialects of Hindi, such as Avadhi, Rajasthani, Brajbhasha, Kosali, Bhojpuri, with elements also from Panjabi and Bengali.

8. I have not included Sufism in this discussion, because I tend to agree with W. H. McLeod that "Muslim beliefs, both Sufi and orthodox, had at most a marginal effect" (*The Evolution of the Sikh Community* (Oxford: Clarendon Press, 1976), p. 6). Important also is the fact that Sufism never really questioned Islam itself: Most Sufis saw themselves as good Muslims. This attachment to a religious label is precisely what is denied by the *sants* and Kabir. Thus, though Sufism was quickly Indianized and was very tolerant towards non-Muslims, it never really questioned the authority of Islam. This is not to say that there were no liberal-minded Sufis, highly regarded by both Muslims and Hindus; for example, Sheikh Farid (whose verses appear in the *Adi Granth*), Sheikh Nizam-ud-Din Auliya, and Madho Lal Hussain.

9. See Harbans Singh, *The Heritage of the Sikhs* (Bombay: Asia Publishing House, 1964); Khushwant Singh, *A History of the Sikhs*, Vol. 1. (Delhi: Oxford University Press, 1977); C. H. Loehlin, *The Sikhs and Their Book* (Lucknow: Lucknow Publishing House, 1946); Sher Singh, *Philosophy of Sikhism* (Lahore, 1944; rpt. New Delhi: Sterling Publishers, 1966); C. G. Narang, *Transformation of Sikhism* (Lahore, 1912; rpt. New Delhi: New Book Society of India, 1960); H. R. Gupta, *Studies in Later Mughal History of the Punjab* (Lahore: Minerva, 1944). McLeod (1976), pp. 1–19, disagrees with this three-fold breakdown and calls it an "oversimplification."

10. Chronologically, the ten Sikh gurus were as follows: Guru Nanak, Guru Angad (1539–1552), Guru Amar Das (1479–1574), Guru Ram Das (1534–1581), Guru Arjan Dev, Guru Har Gobind (1595–1644), Guru Har Rai (1630–1661), Guru Har Krishan (1656–1664), Guru Tegh Bahadur (1621–1675), and Guru Gobind Singh.

11. Jahangir mentions this incident as follows in his autobiography:

"In Gobindwal, which is on the river Biyah (Beas), there was a Hindu named Arjun, in the garments of sainthood and sanctity, so much so that he had captured many of the simple-hearted of the Hindus, and even of the ignorant and foolish followers of Islam, by his ways and manners, and they loudly sounded the drum of his holiness. They called him *Guru*, and from all sides stupid people crowded to worship and manifest complete faith in him. For three or four generations (of spiritual successors) they had kept this shop warm. Many times it occurred to me to put a stop to this vain affair or to bring him into the assembly of the people of Islam.

At last when Khusrau passed along this road this insignificant fellow proposed to wait upon him. Khusrau happened to halt at the place where he was, and he came out and did homage to him. He behaved to Khusrau in certain special ways, and made on his forehead a finger-mark in saffron, which the Indians (Hinduwan) call *qashqa,* and is considered propitious. When this came to my ears and I clearly understood his folly, I ordered them to produce him and handed over his houses, dwelling-places, and children to Murtaza Khan, and having confiscated his property commanded that he should be put to death."

(The Tuzuk-i-Jahangiri or Memoirs of Jahangir, trans. Alexander Rogers, ed. Henry Beveridge [1909–1914; rpt. New Delhi: Munshiram Manoharlal Publishers, 1978], pp. 72–73).

12. Macauliffe states that part of Guru Arjan's last message to Har Gobind was, "Let him sit fully armed on his throne, and maintain an army to the best of his ability" (Macauliffe, vol. 3, p. 99). But Khushwant Singh (1977), Vol. 1, p. 61, questions the authenticity of this tradition.

13. See W. Owen Cole & Piara Singh Sambhi, *The Sikhs: Their Religious Beliefs and Practices* (London: Routledge & Kegan Paul, 1978), pp. 43–52 for a fuller discussion of the role of the Mohan *pothis* in the compilation of the *Adi Granth.*

14. Indian music is based on the idea of moods or *rasas* (literally, "flavors"). Each musical structure (*raga*) can engender countless tunes, and each has various significances, such as the time of day, the season of the year, a particular color, a mood. See René Daumal, *Rasa* trans. Louise Landes Levi (New York: New Directions, 1982) for a good discussion of Indian musical aesthetics.

15. Guru Gobind Singh's own writings are preserved in the *Dasam Granth.* It is made up of eighteen quite different works, which can be roughly divided into reworking mythology, philosophy, autobiography, and erotic poetry. It is said that Guru Gobind Singh himself called all his works mere "word games" and therefore always refused to incorporate them into the body of the *Adi Granth.*

16. See Surindar Singh Kohli, *A Critical Study of the Adi Granth* (New Delhi: Punjabi Writers' Co-operative, 1961), pp. 2–8; Khushwant Singh (1977), pp. 304–309; W. H. McLeod, *Early Sikh Tradition: A Study of the Janam-Sakhis* (Oxford: Clarendon Press, 1980), Appendix 7.

17. See Vaudeville, "Introduction" (1974), p. 58; R. K. Varma, *Sant Kabir* (Allahabad: Sahitya Bhavan, 1966), pp. 25–30; Karine Schomer (1979), p. 76.

18. Shah, "Introduction" (1977), p. 1.

19. Vaudeville, "Introduction" (1974), p. 48.

20. See Vaudeville (1974), pp. 27–48, for the issues in this debate.

21. See K. N. Dvivedi, *Kabir Aur Kabir Panth* (Prayag: Hindi Sahitya Sammelan, Sm. 2022 [1965]), p. 60; Laihana Singh, *Kabir Kasauti* (Bombay: Lakshimivenkateshvar Press, 1962), p. 22.

22. K. N. Dvivedi (1965), p. 60.

23. Laihana Singh (1962), p. 3.

24. *Vikrami* dates are 57 years earlier on the Christian calendar.

25. See Vaudeville (1974), p. 32, note 2.

26. For a discussion of *julahas* and Kabir, see Vaudeville (1974), pp. 81ff; H. P. Dvivedi, *Kabir* (Bombay: Hindi Granth Ratnakar, 1964), pp. 3ff. Interesting also is Herbert Risley, *The People of India* (Calcutta: Thacker & Spink, 1915).

27. For language-games, see the later philosophy of Ludwig Wittgenstein in *Philosophical Investigations*, ed. G. E. M. Anscombe and R. Rhees (Oxford: Blackwell, 1953).

28. See Hess and Singh (1983), pp. 135ff. for a discussion of this rhetorical strategy, examples of *ultvansi* songs in the *Adi Granth* are *Gauri* 14; *Acrostic* "PH" (28) *Asa* 6; *Asa* 22; *Sorath* 6; *Basant* 3.

29. See for example, S. Dasgupta, *Obscure Religious Cults as Background of Bengali Literature* (Calcutta: University of Calcutta, 1946), p. 423; Dvivedi (1964), pp. 80–94; P. D. Barthwal, *Traditions of Indian Mysticism Based on Nirguna School of Hindi Poetry* (New Delhi: Heritage Publishers, 1978), pp. 301ff.

30. Hess and Singh (1983), p. 135.

31. Hess and Singh (1983), p. 194, n. 1.

32. *Meister Eckhart: The Essential Sermons, Commentaries, Treatises, and Defence*, trans., Edmund Colledge and Bernard McGinn (New York: Paulist Press, 1981), 202.

33. The edition of the *Adi Granth* that I am using is *Adi Sri Guru Granth Sahib Ji*, ed. Gyani Mohindar Singh "Ratan" (Amritsar: Bhai Chatar Singh Jivan Singh Pustakanwale, n.d.).

34. This translation is based on *Rgveda with Commentaries*, eds. Vishva Bandhu et al. (Hoshiarpur: Vishveshvaranand Vedic Research Institute, 1963), Part II, "Mandala I.164.45," p. 1072.

35. From "The Task of the Translator," in Walter Benjamin, *Illuminations*, trans. Harry Zohn, ed. Hannah Arendt (New York: Schocken Books, 1969), p. 78.

Bibliography

Panjabi (Gurmukhi):

Adi Sri Guru Granth Sahib Ji, ed. Gyani Mohindar Singh "Ratan." Amritsar: Bhai Chatar Singh Jivan Singh Pustakanwale, n.d.

Kala Singh Bedi. *Guru Nanak Darshan.* New Delhi: Panjabi Parkashan, 1965.

Sarup Dass Bhalla. *Mahima Prakash.* Patiala: Languages Department, 1971.

Gobind Dass. *Shri Guru Granth Sahib.* Amritsar: Manmohan Press, n.d.

Sewa Dass. *Parchai.* Patiala: Bhasha Vibhag, 1963.

Gyan Singh Gyani. *Twarikh Guru Khalsa.* Sialkot: Guru Gobind Singh Press, 1891.

Kahan Singh Nabha. *Mahan Kosh (Guru Shabad Ratanakar).* Patiala: Bhasha Vibhag, 1926.

Piara Singh, ed. *Guru Granth Vichar Kosh.* Patiala: Panjabi University, 1969.

Sahib Singh. *Guru Arjan Dev.* Amritsar: Singh Brothers, 1967.

———. *Shri Guru Granth Sahib Darpan.* Jallandhar: Raj Publishers, n.d.

Taran Singh. *Bhagti te Shakti.* Amritsar: Bhai Fakir Singh & Sons, 1962.

———. *Shri Guru Granth Sahib da Sahatik Itihas.* Amritsar: Shromani Gurdwara Parbandhak Committee, 1968.

Kartar Singh Suri. *Guru Arjan Dev te Sant Dadu Dayal.* Chandigarh: Panjabi Lekhak Madan, 1969.

Hindi:

P. D. Barthwal. *Gorakhbani*. Prayag: Hindi Sahitya Sammelan, 1942.

H. P. Dvivedi. *Kabir*. Bombay: Hindi Granth Ratnakar, 1964.

————. *Nath Siddhon ki Baniyan*. Benares: Sahitya Bhandar, 1957.

K. N. Dvivedi. *Kabir aur Kabir Panth*. Prayag: Hindi Sahitya Sammelan, 1965.

B. N. Mishra. *Sant Sahitya aur Sadhana*. New Delhi: National Publishing House, 1969.

R. Raghava. *Gorakhnath aur unka Yug*. New Delhi: Atmaram & Sons, 1963.

Laihana Singh. *Kabir Kasauti*. Bombay: Lakshmivenkateshvar Press, 1962.

R. D. Singh. *Santon ka Bhakti Yoga*. Varanasi: Bharatiya Vidya Prakashan, 1968.

B. N. Tiwari. *Kabir: Jivan aur Darshan*. Allahabad: Sahitya Bhavan, 1978.

P. N. Tiwari. *Kabir Vani Samgraha*. Allahabad: Lokbharati Parkashan, 1970.

R. K. Varma. *Sant Kabir*. Allahabad: Sahitya Bhavan, 1966.

Translations of the Adi Granth:

M. A. Macauliffe. *The Sikh Religion*. 1909; rpt. New Delhi: S. Chand & Company, 1983.

Gopal Singh, trans. *Sri Guru Granth Sahib*. New Delhi: Gurdas Kapur & Sons, 1962.

Manmohan Singh, trans. *Sri Guru Granth Sahib*. Amritsar: Shromani Gurdwara Parbandhak Committee, 1962–1969.

Gurbachan Singh Talib, trans. *Sri Guru Granth Sahib*. 2 Vols. Patiala: Punjabi University, 1985.

E. Trumpp, trans. *The Adi-Granth*. 1877; rpt. New Delhi: Munshiram Manhorlal, 1970.

Selections from the Adi Granth:

Gobind Singh Mansukhi. *Hymns from the Holy Granth*. New Delhi: Hemkunt Press, 1975.

Selections from the Sacred Writings of the Sikhs. UNESCO. Allen & Unwin, 1966.

Khushwant Singh. *The Hymns of Guru Nanak*. Calcutta: Orient Longmans, 1972.

General Works:

A. J. Appaswamy. *The Theology of Hindu Bhakti*. Indian Theological Library, No. 5. Banglore: Christian Literature Society Press, 1970.

A. J. Arberry. *Muslim Saints and Mystics*. Chicago: University of Chicago Press, 1966.

John C. Archer. *The Sikhs in Relation to Hindus, Muslims, Christians and Ahmadiyyas*. Princeton, N.J.: Princeton University Press, 1946.

S. S. Bal. *Guru Nanak and His Times*. Chandigarh: Punjab University, 1969.

A. Bannerjee. *Guru Nanak and His Times*. Patiala: Punjabi University, 1971.

A. K. Bannerjee. *The Philosophy of Gorakhnath*. Gorakhpur: Mahant Dig Vijai Nath Trust, 1961.

N. Gerald Barrier. *The Sikhs and Their Literature*. New Delhi: Manohar Book Service, 1970.

N. Gerald Barrier and Harbans Singh, eds. *Punjab Past and Present: Essays in Honor of Dr. Ganda Singh*. Patiala: Panjabi University Press, 1976.

P. D. Barthwal. *The Nirguna School of Hindi Poetry*. Benares: Indian Book Shop, 1936.

B. Behari. *Sufis, Mystics and Yogis of India*. Bombay: Bharatiya Vidya Bhavan, 1962.

A. Bharati. *The Tantric Tradition.* New York: Doubleday and Co., 1970.

Narendra Nath Bhattacharyya. *History of the Sakta Religion.* New Delhi: Munshiram Manoharlal, 1974.

G. W. Briggs. *Gorakhnath and the Kanphata Yogis.* Calcutta: Y.M.C.A. Publishing House, 1938.

Krishna Chaitanya. *Sanskrit Poetics.* Bombay: Asia Publishing House, 1965.

P. C. Chakravati. *Doctrine of Sakti in Indian Literature.* Calcutta: General Printers and Publishers Ltd., 1940.

Prem Chand, trans. *A Translation of Kabir's Complete Bijak into English.* Calcutta: Baptist Mission, 1911.

R. Chaudhuri. *Sufism and Vedanta.* Calcutta: Pracyavani Mandir, 1945–1948.

W. Owen Cole. *The Guru in Sikhism.* London: Darton, Longman & Todd, 1982.

———. *Sikhism in Its Indian Context.* London: Darton, Longman & Todd, 1982.

W. Owen Cole and Piara Singh Sambhi. *The Sikhs: Their Religious Beliefs and Practices.* London: Routledge & Kegan Paul, 1978.

Alain Danielou. *Hindu Polytheism.* New York: Pantheon Books, 1964.

S. B. Dasgupta. *Obscure Religious Cults as Background of Bengali Literature.* Calcutta: University of Calcutta, 1946.

———. *An Introduction to Tantric Buddhism.* Calcutta: University of Calcutta, 1958.

S. N. Dasgupta. *Hindu Mysticism.* New York: Frederick Ungar Publishing Co., 1967.

Bhagat Lachman Dass. *Sikh Martyrs.* Madras: Ganesh & Co., 1923.

René Daumal. *Rasa.* Trans. Louise Landes Levi. New York: New Directions, 1982.

Edward C. Dimock, Jr. *The Place of the Hidden Moon.* Chicago: University of Chicago Press, 1966.

I. A. Ezekiel. *Kabir the Great Mystic.* Beas, Panjab: Radha Soami Satsang, 1966.

Peter Fripp. *The Mystic Philosophy of the Sant Mat.* London: Neville Spearman Ltd., 1964.

J. Gonda. *Visnuism and Sivaism.* London: Athlone Press, 1970.

B. K. Goswami. *The Bhakti Cult in Ancient India.* Varanasi: Chowk-hamba Sanskrit Series, 1965.

B. N. Goswamy and J. S. Grewal. *The Mughal and Sikh Rulers and the Vaishnavas of Pindori.* Simla: Indian Institute of Advanced Study, 1969.

Duncan Greenlees. *The Gospel of the Guru-Granth Sahib.* Madras: Theosophical Publishing House, 1960.

J. S. Grewal. *Guru Nanak in History.* Chandigarh: Punjab University, 1969.

———. *From Guru Nanak to Maharaja Ranjit Singh.* Amritsar: Guru Nanak University, 1972.

———. *The Present State of Sikh Studies.* Batala: Christian Institute of Sikh Studies, 1973.

H. R. Gupta. Studies in *Later Mughal History of the Punjab.* Lahore: Minerva, 1944.

Eric Gustafson and Kenneth Jones. *Sources on Punjab History.* New Delhi: Manohar, 1975.

M. A. Hanifi. *Jainism.* Patiala: Punjabi University, 1970.

Linda Hess and Shukdev Singh, trans. *The Bijak of Kabir.* San Francisco: North Point Press, 1983.

Mark Juergensmeyer and N. Gerald Barrier, eds. *Sikh Studies: Comparative Perspectives on a Changing Tradition.* Berkeley, Calif.: Berkeley Graduate Theological Union Religious Studies Series, 1979.

K. L. Kalla. *The Influence of Yoga Philosophy on Hindi Poetry*. Dehra Dun: Sahitya Sadan, 1967.

Frank Ernest Keay. *Kabir and His Followers*. New Delhi: Association Press, 1931.

Surindar Singh Kohli. *A Critical Study of the Adi Granth*. New Delhi: Punjabi Writers' Co-operative, 1961.

Per Kvaerne. *An Anthology of Buddhist Tantric Songs*. Oslo: Norwegian Research Council, 1977.

C. H. Loehlin. *The Sikhs and Their Book*. Lucknow: Lucknow Publishing House, 1946.

————. *The Sikhs and Their Scriptures*. Lucknow: Lucknow Publishing House, 1958.

————. *The Granth of Guru Gobind Singh and the Khalsa Brotherhood*. Lucknow: Lucknow Publishing House, 1971.

M. A. Macauliffe. *The Sikh Religion*. 6 vols. 1909; rpt. New Delhi: S. Chand & Company Ltd., 1983.

W. H. McLeod. *Guru Nanak and the Sikh Religion*. Oxford: Clarendon Press, 1968.

————. *The Evolution of the Sikh Community*. Oxford: Clarendon Press, 1976.

————. *Early Sikh Tradition: A Study of the Janam-Sakhis*. Oxford: Clarendon Press, 1980.

Clarence O. McMullen, ed. *The Nature of Guruship*. Batala: Christian Institute of Sikh Studies, 1976.

Gokul Chand Narang. *Transformation of Sikhism*. Lahore, 1912; rpt. New Delhi: New Book Society of India, 1960.

Kirpal Narang. *History of the Punjab*. New Delhi: Uttar Chand Kapur and Sons, 1964.

B. S. Nijjar. *Punjab under the Later Mughals*. Jalandhar: New Academic Publishing Co., 1972.

W. G. Orr. *A Sixteenth-Century Indian Mystic*. London: Lutterworth Press, 1947.

Ishwari Prasad. *A History of Medieval India*. Allahabad: The Indian Press, 1966.

Niharranjan Ray. *The Sikh Gurus and the Sikh Society*. New Delhi: Munshiram Manoharlal Publishers Ltd., 1975.

Louis Renou and Jean Filliozat. *L'Inde classique: Manuel des études indiennes*. 3 vols. Paris: Imprimerie Nationale, 1947–1953.

Karine Schomer. "Kabir in the *Guru Granth Sahib:* An Exploratory Essay." In *Sikh Studies: Comparative Perspectives on a Changing Tradition*. Ed. Mark Juergensmeyer and N. Gerald Barrier.

Karine Schomer and W. H. McLeod, eds. *The Sant Traditions of India*. Berkeley, Calif.: Berkeley Graduate Theological Union Religious Studies Series, 1983.

Ahmad Shah, trans. *The Bijak of Kabir*. Hamirpur, 1917; rpt. New Delhi: Asian Publication Services, 1979.

Avtar Singh. *Ethics of the Sikhs*. Patiala: Punjabi University, 1970.

Dalip Singh. *Yoga and Sikh Teachings: Some Basic Questions*. Chandigarh: Bahri Publications, 1979.

Darshan Singh. *Indian Bhakti Tradition and the Sikh Gurus*. Chandigarh: Lyall Book Depot, 1968.

Fauja Singh. *Historians and Historiography of the Sikhs*. New Delhi, 1978.

———. *Development of Sikhism under the Gurus*. Patiala: Punjabi University, 1982.

Ganda Singh. *Bibliography of the Punjab*. Patiala: Punjabi University, 1966.

———. *Sources on the Life and Teachings of Guru Nanak*. Patiala: Punjabi University, 1969.

Gurdev Singh. *Perspectives on the Sikh Tradition*. Patiala: Academy of Sikh Religion and Culture, 1986.

Harbans Singh. *The Heritage of the Sikhs*. Bombay: Asia Publishing House, 1964.

————. *Guru Nanak and the Origins of the Sikh Faith*. Bombay: Asia Publishing House, 1969.

————, ed. *Perspectives on Guru Nanak*. Patiala: Punjabi University, 1975.

Khushwant Singh. *A History of the Sikhs*. 2 vols. New Delhi: Oxford University Press, 1977.

Mohan Singh. *A History of Punjabi Literature, 1100–1932*. Amritsar: Kasturi Lal and Sons, 1956.

Puran Singh. *The Book of the Ten Masters*. Patiala: Punjabi University, 1981.

Sher Singh. *Philosophy of Sikhism*. Lahore, 1944; rpt. New Delhi: Sterling Publishers, 1966.

Taran Singh. *Teachings of Guru Nanak*. Patiala: Punjabi University, 1977.

————. *Guru Nanak and Indian Religious Thought*. Patiala: Punjabi University, 1981.

————. *Sikh Gurus and Indian Spiritual Thought*. Patiala: Punjabi University, 1981.

Teja Singh. *The Psalm of Peace*. Amritsar: Khalsa Brother, 1937.

————. *Sikhism: Its Ideals and Institutions*. Calcutta: Orient Longman, 1964.

Teja Singh and Ganda Singh. *A Short History of the Sikhs*. Bombay: Orient Longman, 1950.

Trilochan Singh. *Guru Nanak: Founder of Sikhism*. New Delhi: Shromani Gurdwara Parbandhak Committee, 1969.

John A. Subhan. *Sufism: Its Saints and Shrines*. Lucknow: Lucknow Publishing House, 1960.

Rabindranath Tagore and Evelyn Underhill. *One Hundred Poems of Kabir*. Calcutta: Macmillan, 1915.

Charlotte Vaudeville, trans. *Kabir Granthavali (Doha)*. Pondicherry: Institut Français d'Indologie, 1957.

————. *Au Cabaret de l'amour: Paroles de Kabir.* Paris: Gallimard, 1959.

————. *Kabir I.* Oxford: Clarendon Press, 1974.

A. K. Warder. *Indian Buddhism.* New Delhi: Motilal Banarsidass, 1970.

John C. B. Webster, ed. *Popular Religion in the Punjab Today.* Batala: Christian Institute of Sikh Studies, 1974.

G. H. Westcott. *Kabir and the Kabir Panth.* Cawnpore: Christ Church Mission Press, 1907.

*Songs of Kabir from
the Adi Granth*

From Shri Raga

1

A mother watching
her son grow
does not realize
that day by day
his life lessens.
With great love
she says, "My son, my dear son" —
Raja Yama looks on and laughs.

You have cast the world
into illusion;
enraptured by Maya,
how can it understand? (Rest)

Kabir says,
"Forsake worldly pleasures,
which harbor certain death.
O living creatures,
praise Ram:
His word gives life eternal —
in this way you will cross over
this world's ocean.

"If He wishes,
you will learn to love Him:
Falsehood and doubt will then
flee from inside you;
you will be calm,
your mind will be illumined —
by the guru's grace
you will be filled with love."

When you reach this state
there is no dying:
Obey His command
and meet the Master. (Rest)

2

Hey pundit! Listen to this marvel;
I can't describe it:
gods, men, Shiva's devotees, the celestial dancers,
are all in love with Maya;
the three worlds are ensnared in her noose.

Raja Ram's lyre plays without being touched;
they, on whom He looks with grace, love its music. (Rest)

My brain is the furnace,
the two flues, the golden tub,
in which I have placed the One.
In that tub drips pure ambrosia—
far more delicious than all nectars.

And here's another marvel:
I have made breath my cup.
In the three worlds,
He is the only Yogi.
Tell me, now, who's the real raja?

Such is Purushotama's knowledge
that Kabir says, "I am drenched in its color.
All the world is lost in falsehood—
my soul is drunk
in the tavern of ambrosia."

From Raga Gauri

1

Burning, I found Ram's water:
it cooled my flaming body. (Rest)

Though you go to forests
to kill your ego —
you will never find Bhagwan
without this water.

Fire burned
both gods and men —
Ram's water saved
His slaves.

Amidst this world's ocean
is a pool of solace;
though you drink from it forever,
it never dries up.

Kabir says,
"Praise Sarangpani;
the water of Ram
has quenched my thirst."

2

O Madho, thirst for water is unending:
the more I drink, the higher flares fire. (Rest)

You are the water-hoard —
I, a fish in that water.

I live in water:
without water, there is death.

You are the cage—
I, a little parrot of yours:
how can that cat Yama
harm me?

You are the tree—
I, a little bird:
Unfortunate are those
who fail to see You.

You are the True Guru—
I, a newly made disciple:
Kabir says, "Come, meet me—
even in this last hour."

3

When I understood the One
to be all-pervasive—
why did people
get annoyed?

I am honorless, without shame;
none need follow my course. (Rest)

If I am wicked
then evil is in my heart only;
you don't have to
associate with me.

My honor or dishonor
brings you no shame;
you'll find out
when your own pretensions are laid bare.

Kabir says,
"All honor belongs to Hari.

Forsake all,
and worship Ram."

4

If by roaming around naked
you can find God,
then all the forest-animals
should have been saved.

Why go naked or wear skins
when you can't see Ram in your own heart. (Rest)

If by shaving your head
you gain spiritual fulfillment,
why aren't all the sheep
saved?

If by holding back sperm
you acquire salvation, my friend,
why haven't eunuchs achieved
that highest condition of the soul?

Kabir says,
"Listen, O men, my brothers,
who ever received salvation
without Ram's name?"

5

Those ritually bathing
day and night
are like frogs
in water.

Without love for Ram's name in their hearts,
they are all in the power of Dharmraja. (Rest)

Those who love their bodies
put on many adornments;

they know no mercy—
not even in their dreams.

The learned read
all the four Vedas;
but only sages will acquire
solace in this sea of affliction.

Kabir says,
"Why are you pondering so deeply?
Give up everything
and drink the best of nectars."

6

What use is prayer,
penance, worship,
when your heart
loves another?

Friend, tie yourself to Madho;
you can't meet Chaturbhuj through wisdom alone. (Rest)

Toss aside greed
and people-pleasing;
throw away lust,
anger, and pride.

Religious practices
tie people down with self-pride:
They all get together
and worship a stone.

Kabir says,
"I found Him through devotion;
by becoming simple-hearted
I met Raghurai."

7

You don't know your caste
when you're in the womb.
All are born
from Brahma's seed.

Say, pundit, when did you become a Brahmin?
Don't waste your life saying, "I'm a Brahmin." (Rest)

If you are a Brahmin,
born of a Brahmin mother,
then why weren't you born
by some other method?

How are you a Brahmin?
How are we Sudras?
How are we of blood?
How are you of milk?

Kabir says,
"He who meditates on Brahma
is a Brahmin,
in my opinion."

8

No one can sleep
in pitch darkness:
raja or beggar
both would cry out.

If your tongue does not say "Ram,"
you will always weep over birth, death. (Rest)

As you see
a tree's shadow —
so breath leaves. Tell me,
to whom does wealth really belong?

As sound pervades
a musical instrument—
so how can you know
the secret of departed souls?

Like a swan on a lake—
so death upon a body.
Drink from Ram's hoard
of ambrosia, O Kabir.

9

Light's creation—
creation's light,
on which blossom fruits
of glass or pearl.

Which house is really safe
where you can dwell without fear? (Rest)

You cannot have inner peace
by bathing on holy river banks;
even there people are busy
with good deeds and bad.

Good and bad deeds
are both the same—
the philosopher's stone is in your very house:
Forget all other merits.

Kabir, forget not the name
of the Formless One;
stay absorbed
in this pastime.

10

Those who say they know Him
who is beyond thought and conception,
hope to go to heaven
by merely saying so.

I don't know where heaven is. Everyone
says, "I'm going there, I'm going there." (Rest)

There is no comfort
in saying this.
Your heart can only be happy
when pride leaves you.

As long as you yearn
for heaven,
you cannot live
near His feet.

Kabir says, "How can I understand
it enough to explain:
Heaven is found
in the company of sages."

11

Birth, growth,
maturity, destruction:
With your own eyes
you see the world pass away.

Die not shamefully saying,
"This house is mine."
In the end,
nothing is really yours. (Rest)

With endless care
you nursed your body:
When you died,
it was burned with fire.

With perfume and sandal-wood lotions
you massaged your limbs:
Your body was burned
in a pile of wood.

Kabir says,
"Listen, O philosopher,
the world can only see
perishable forms."

12

Why mourn
when someone dies?
It would be fitting only
if we had to stay alive forever.

I shall not die like the rest:
I have met the Giver of life. (Rest)

You perfume your body
with many fragrances;
in all these delights,
you forget the highest bliss.

There is one little well,
and five water-carriers;
though the hoist is broken,
they still draw water.

Kabir, say,
"When meditation awakens,
there is neither the little well
nor the water-carriers."

13

The stationary, the moving,
the crawling, the flying—
through all these many births
have I come.

I have lived in many bodies, O Ram,
as I wandered from birth to birth. (Rest)

A yogi, an ascetic,
a penitent, a student—
I was even a king under an umbrella,
or a beggar.

Those distant, die;
saints all live.
Lick Ram's nectar
with your tongue.

Kabir, say,
"Prabhu, have mercy;
I am weary;
save me."

14

Kabir, I have seen strange sights:
Water, mistaken for milk, being churned; (Rest)

a donkey eating a green grape-vine,
and then laughing and killing himself braying;

a drunken bullock going about unchecked,
romping and grazing and going to hell.

Kabir, say, "The sport is revealed:
The sheep forever suckling the lamb."

By pondering upon Ram, the mind is illumined;
Kabir, say, "The Guru has given me realization."

15

Like a fish forsaking water
and coming out on dry land,
I did no penance
in all my previous lives.

Now, Ram, tell me, what's going to happen?
Was I foolish to leave Benares? (Rest)

You squandered all your life
in Shiva's city;
and now at the time of death,
you've moved to Magahar;

you worshipped so many years
in Benares;
now that you're dying
you go live in Magahar;

you consider Benares and Magahar
to be the same;
with such half-cooked devotion,
how will you cross over?

I say, all men recognize
Ganesha and Shiva;
but Kabir, even dead,
remembers the Lord Ram.

16

Limbs massaged with perfume
and sandal-oil—
and then they burn that body
on a pile of wood.

Where are the splendors of body, of wealth?
They remain on earth; they can't go with you. (Rest)

People sleep at night,
work by day,
not uttering Hari's name
even for a moment.

A kite-string in their hands,
betel leaf in their mouths;
when they die,
they are tied tight like thieves.

Those who, guided by their guru's wisdom,
sing of Hari with pleasure,
obtain solace
by remembering only Ram.

In the heart where, in His mercy,
He places His name,
there exudes
the sweet fragrance of Hari, Hari.

Kabir says, "Hey, blindman
think:
Ram is truth,
all work is false."

17

Yama has turned into Ram;
sorrow has fled, solace taken hold.
Enemies have turned into friends;
the godless have turned into saints.

All bliss is now revealed to me:
I became peaceful when I saw Gobind. (Rest)

My body had a million afflictions—
they all turned into eternal joy.
Learn to recognize your own self,
and sickness, the three fevers will not touch you.

Now my heart has turned primordial;
I understood, by dying while still alive.
Kabir, say, "I have blended with bliss;
I am not afraid, nor do I frighten others."

18

When the body dies,
where does the soul go?
The guru's word says

it blends with the unmoving, endless One.
Those who know Ram
can easily understand—
like a mute man savoring sugar.

Banwari is unveiling knowledge:
O my soul, gather your breath
at the windpipe's node. (Rest)

Find that Guru
who makes all others useless.
Enjoy that pleasure
which dulls all others.
Acquire that knowledge
which darkens all others.
Die in such a way
that you may not see death again.

I have reversed the Ganges
and fused it with the Jamuna:
at the confluence of my heart
I bathe where there is no water.
My eyes see everyone as equal—
that is my way.
When you meditate upon truth,
why think of other things?

Water, fire,
air, earth, sky:
Like all these,
I live close to Hari.
Kabir, say,
"I remember Niranjan.
I have gone to that house
from which I will not come out."

19

Measures of pure gold cannot buy Him:
By selling my heart I purchased Ram.

I know now that Ram is my very own;
my heart searches no longer for solace. (Rest)

My devotion leads to my house that same Ram
for whom Brahma's description could find no end.

Kabir, say, "I am wayward no longer:
Ram's service is now my lot."

20

Death, which frightens
the whole world,
is revealed to me in its reality
by the guru's word.

How can I die now: I've accepted death.
Those who do not know Ram die forever. (Rest)

Everyone talks
of death and dying;
those who die calmly
are immortal.

Kabir, say,
"My heart is blissful:
Superstition flees,
supreme solace remains."

21

Nowhere can I find
a place to rub on salve;
I can find no hurt,
though I look hard.

Only they who feel it know pain.
Devotion for Ram is a sharp arrow. (rest)

I see all women
with love.

But how can I know
which of them is loved by her husband.

Kabir says,
"The Bridegroom will come and embrace her
who has goodness inside,
forsaking all others."

22

Endlessly salvation
calls out to those
who have Hari
as their master, O my brother.

O Ram, my hope is in You—
I am obliged to no one. (Rest)

Why should He not
nourish me,
who bears the weight
of the three worlds.

Kabir, say,
"Here's some wisdom I've thought up:
If your own mother gives you poison,
what can you do?"

23

Without truth,
how can a woman be a suttee?
Hey, pundit, behold
and think in your heart.

How can you love without love?
You can't love if you savor Maya's pleasures. (Rest)

They who hold Maya
to be the true queen in their heart

cannot meet Ram
even in their dreams.

"She who yields her body,
her heart, wealth, home,
is the true enraptured wife,"
says Kabir.

24

The whole world
is enthralled by Maya;
this same Maya
has drowned whole families.

O man, how did you wreck
your raft in such a wide, clear place?
Because you broke away from Hari,
and hooked on to Maya.

Gods and men burn;
the fire blazes.
Water is so near,
yet the beasts don't drink.

By meditating, by meditating,
the water sprang forth.
"That water is pure,"
says Kabir.

25

If, in a family, no son
meditates upon divine wisdom—
better the mother
had been barren.

Why didn't the man who never served Ram
die a sinner right at birth? (Rest)

Many wombs miscarry;
how was he saved?
He lives like a cripple
in the world.

Kabir, say,
"The beautiful, the handsome,
are ugly hunchbacks,
without His name."

26

I am a sacrifice to those
who utter the Master's name.

Pure are they who exalt the pure Hari:
They are my brothers, dear to my heart. (Rest)

I am the dust of their flower-like feet
whose hearts spill over with Ram.

I'm a weaver by caste, patient by heart:
Slowly, slowly Kabir celebrates His virtues.

27

The sky is my still
from which drips luscious ambrosia.
I made my body firewood
to brew this choicest of liquors.

Call them forever drunk
who drink Ram's vintage
by meditating upon wisdom. (Rest)

Ever since I met up
with this steadfast barmaid,
each of my days
passes in blissful drunkenness.

While savoring this bliss
I turned my mind on Niranjan;
Kabir, say,
"I found illumination."

28

The nature of your heart
determines your mind:
So how can you be enlightened
if you smother your heart?

Which ascetic has ever immolated his heart?
Tell me, who ever swam across by strangling his heart. (Rest)

People speak
what is in their hearts—
but you cannot know devotion
without first stifling your heart.

Kabir, say,
"Those who know the secret
become like Madhusudan,
the Preserver of the three worlds."

29

All these stars
that I see in the sky,
which painter
painted them?

Say, pundit, what's the sky knotted to?
Only the wise can unravel that. (Rest)

Sun and moon
give light;
all things are suffused
with the light of Brahma.

Kabir, say,
"Only they will know
in whose hearts is Ram,
on whose tongues is Ram."

30

The daughter of the Vedas
is Smriti, O my brothers;
she has brought with her
a chain and a rope.

She has leashed her own city
with love's snare, and drawn death's arrow. (Rest)

The knot cannot be cut;
it does not break.
It has become a snake
that eats away the world.

I have seen her loot
the entire earth.
Kabir, say,
"I broke free by saying 'Ram.' "

31

Placing a bit and bridle
to my heart,
I race across the sky,
forsaking all else.

Thought is my saddle:
I place my foot in the stirrup of peace. (Rest)

Come on, let me take you
to Heaven;
if you rear, I'll lash you
with love's whip.

Kabir, say,
"Only they are good horse-riders
who keep far away
from holy books."

32

I have seen the mouth that ate all
the five ambrosias being set on fire.

Burning by fire, hanging in the womb—
my precious Ram, remove these pains. (Rest)

A body is destroyed in many ways:
Some burn it, others bury it in earth.

Kabir, say, "Hari, show me Your feet:
Afterwards send Yama if You wish."

33

He is fire, He is wind;
the Master has started the fire—
who can put it out?

Let my body burn; I am praising Ram.
My heart has blended with Ram's name. (Rest)

Who is burned? Who is injured?
Sarangpani plays
so many roles.

Kabir says, "Utter these words:
If You are the Master,
You will save me."

34

I have never paid attention
to the discipline of Yoga:

Without renunciation
you cannot escape Maya.

How can we stand if we do not have
Ram's name as our pillar? (Rest)

Kabir, say,
"I have searched as far as the sky—
but have found none equal
to Ram."

35

The head on which
a turban was tied with great care
is now being rearranged by ravens' beaks.

Why be proud of this body and wealth?
Why not gain security in Ram's name? (Rest)

Kabir says, "Listen, O my heart—
the same thing
is going to happen to you."

From Raga Gauri-Guareri

36

When I ask for solace,
I am given pain.
I was not asking
for peace such as this.

With Maya on our mind, we hope for solace.
How can we live with Raja Ram? (Rest)

The solace—that even
Shiva and Brahma dreaded—
is the one
I hold worthy.

The four sons of Brahma, and
the saint Narada, and Sheshnaga
never recognized
the soul within their bodies.

Search out this soul,
O my brothers:
when it parts from the body,
where is it absorbed?

By the guru's grace
Jaidev and Namdev
learned about devotion
through love.

The soul will not
come and go again and again.

They, who are deluded
no longer, know the truth.

The soul has no shape
or appearance.
On command it was made,
on command it will be absorbed.

Those who know the soul's secret
will be absorbed
into the Giver of Peace,
by way of the soul.

One Soul;
many bodies:
Kabir, worship
that Soul.

37

Those who stayed awake day and night
to repeat the one Name
became saints
by offering their love. (Rest)

Ascetics and hermits all have failed;
His name alone is the tree
that becomes the raft
and carries us to the other side.

Say, "Hari, Hari,"
and you won't be parted from Him:
Kabir, say,
"I recognize Ram's name."

From Ragas Gauri or Sorath

38

Barefaced soul,
aren't you ashamed?
You've abandoned Hari,
now where are you going? (Rest)

It doesn't suit you
to wander from place to place
if your Master
is high and mighty.

That Master
is all-pervasive:
Hari is ever-present
never far away.

At whose feet even Lakshmi
takes shelter —
tell me, friend,
could anything be lacking in His house?

He whom everyone
talks about
is strong —
our Master and Preserver.

Kabir, say,
"They are pure in the world
in whose hearts
lives no other."

39

Who really has a son?
Who, a father?
Who really dies?
Who can inflict pain?

Trickster-Hari has drugged the world;
but, O my mother, I can't live without Hari. (Rest)

Who really has a husband?
Who, a wife?
Think about this reality
now that you have assumed human shape.

Kabir, say,
"My heart is happy with the Trickster:
The drug has worn off
and I now recognize Him."

40

Raja Ram is now my support:
Casting off birth and death,
I have reached the supreme stage. (Rest)

He has placed me among saints
and saved me from the five sins.
My tongue repeats His sweet name.
He has made me His slave without purchase.

The True Guru did me a favor:
He rescued me from this world's ocean.
I am in love with His ambrosial feet;
Gobind dwells in my thoughts forever.

The glowing spark of Maya's fire is extinguished;
because of His name my heart knows peace.
Prabhu the Master is present in water and earth:
Wherever I look, Antarjami is there.

He Himself made me His devotee. You too can meet Him,
if it is destined, O my brothers.
If He is merciful, you will be successful.
Kabir's Swami is the nourisher of the poor.

41

Impure is water,
impure is earth,
impure is birth.
Impure are all those born;
impure are the dead:
Impurity stains the world.

Hey, pundit, tell me,
who is really pure?
Give me a revelation, my friend. (Rest)

Impure are eyes,
impure is tongue,
impure are ears.
Impure are you
whether standing or sitting:
Impurity defiles kitchens.

Everyone knows
how to get trapped—
few know how to get out.
Kabir, say, "Those who meditate upon Ram
in their hearts
are never impure."

From Raga Gauri

42

Settle this one quarrel, O Ram,
if you want service from Your slave: (Rest)

Is the soul greater,
or that into which it is absorbed?
Is Ram greater,
or those who recognize Him?

Is Brahma greater,
or He who created him?
Are the Vedas greater,
or the Source from which they emerged?

Kabir, say,
"I can't make up my mind
whether pilgrimage is greater
or Hari's slave."

From Raga Gauri-Cheti

43

Look, brothers,
a dust-storm of knowledge has arisen,
blowing away superstition's bamboo screen:
Nothing remains tied down to Maya. (Rest)

It has knocked down doubt's two posts,
and broken worldly love's girder.
Greed's thatched roof has fallen to the ground,
folly's clay-pot has shattered.

Your slave was drenched in the rain
that followed the storm.
Kabir, say, "My heart became radiant
when the sun came out."

44

They neither hear nor sing Hari's praise,
but brag about bringing down
even the sky itself.

What do you say to such people
whom Prabhu has kept so far away?
You should fear them always. (Rest)

They never give even a palmful of water,
yet they curse those who give
like the flowing Ganges.

They ever walk the crooked path.
They have destroyed themselves;
now they seek to destroy others.

They know nothing but slander;
they do not listen —
not even to Brahma.

They themselves are lost
and now cause others to stray:
They sleep in homes set on fire.

They laugh at others,
though they themselves are one-eyed.
Seeing them all Kabir is ashamed.

From Raga Gauri-Bairagan

45

No one cares for their parents
when they are alive—
but when they die, people offer *sradha*.
Tell me, how will the poor parents get
what is being eaten by ravens and dogs.

Someone explain "bliss' to me.
I am tired of hearing "bliss, bliss"—
how do you get this "bliss"? (Rest)

You make goddesses and gods of clay
and then you offer them living sacrifices—
you call these your ancestors
who can't even ask
for what they want?

You cut down living creatures;
you worship lifeless objects:
It will be hard for you in the end.
You never understood the reality of Ram's name;
so you drowned in the sea of fear.

You worship goddesses, gods, and you flounder,
never knowing He who is beyond Brahma.
Kabir says,
"You never thought of the Casteless One,
wrapped up as you were with Maya."

From Raga Gauri

46

Die while you live;
live when you die —
and be absorbed into Silence.
If amidst impurity you remain pure,
you shall not be in this world's ocean again.

O my Ram, churn the milk —
my guru's advice stills my heart,
and I drink ambrosia. (Rest)

Without fitting arrow to bow,
the Guru has rent this world,
O my brother:
Wind carries a kite in all directions,
but the string stays tied to love.

The soul grieved by separation
has been absorbed into Silence;
uncertainty and evil thoughts have fled.
Kabir, say, "I have experienced a miracle
by falling in love with Ram's name."

From Raga Gauri-Bairagan

47

By turning breath upside down,
by stringing together the six spheres,
my mind came to love Silence.
He neither comes nor goes away;
He neither dies nor is born —
search Him out, O Bairagi.

O my soul, turn the heart upside down
and be absorbed in Him.
By the guru's grace my mind has changed;
before I was nothing but a stranger. (Rest)

For them who accept His reality,
things near are far away,
those far away are near:
Like sherbet made from sugar —
only those who drink it
know what it is like.

O Nirgun,
to whom can I tell Your tale?
Who can be so wise?
Kabir, say,
"Only those who ignite
see the flash."

From Raga Gauri

48

Over there,
there is no rain, ocean, sunshine, or shade.
Over there,
there is no creation or destruction,
neither living nor dying,
neither the touch of sorrow or joy.
Over there,
there is neither solitude nor meditation.

Hard to describe that eternal peace:
Over there,
nothing is measured, nothing depleted,
nothing is light, nothing heavy. (Rest)

Over there,
none is high or low.
Over there,
there is neither night nor day.
Over there,
there is neither water, air, nor fire.
Over there,
only the True Guru permeates all.

Unaccessible, beyond thought
is the Eternal One;
He can be found
by the guru's grace.
Kabir, say,
"I sacrifice myself
for my Guru —
may I blend with His true being."

49

You bought the two oxen, Sin and Charity;
you were born with breath as your capital.
In every heart is a sack full of greed —
and a whole herd is bought,
laden with goods.

My Ram is that merchant
who turned everyone into traders. (Rest)

Lust and Wrath are tax-collectors,
the impulses of the heart — bandits.
These, together with the five elements,
plunder the gift,
while laden goods pass by on the other shore.

Kabir says, "Listen, O sages,
this is the present situation:
The one ox became weary
of climbing mountain passes,
and, dropping its load, ran away."

50

For a few days only does a woman
live in her father's home:
Eventually she must go to her in-laws.
Blind people cannot see this;
neither can fools and idiots.

See, the bride stands wearing
only half her dress —
and guests have come already
to take her away. (Rest)

Do you see that well over there?
Who is the girl lowering the hoist?

The bucket has broken
from the rope —
and she who drew water has left.

If her husband is kind and merciful,
she can make amends.
Only she is a contented wife
who remembers her master's words —
learn and recognize.

All others wander around,
tied down to past deeds —
look and think.
Why blame her?
What can the poor woman do?

She got up and left
with hopes unfulfilled —
her mind never knew peace.
Stay close to Hari's feet
and take shelter, O Kabir.

51

Yogis say only yoga is good and sweet
and nothing else, O my brothers.
Bald-pated ascetics and Gosain hermits
say that only they have achieved illumination.

Without Hari, the blind wander in superstition.
Those to whom I went for freedom
were themselves tied down by chains. (Rest)

As the world was created, so it remains:
That's why it is lost in superstition.
Pundits and those virtuous, valiant, generous
say that they are the greatest of all.

Only they can guess to whom He gives the riddle:
How can we live without guessing?

Upon meeting the True Guru, darkness lifts—
come and receive the gem.

Forsake all immoral deeds
and remain secure at Hari's feet.
Kabir, say, "It's like a mute eating sugar—
ask him and what can he say?"

From Raga Gauri-Purabi

52

Where once there was something,
now there is nothing:
Gone are the five elements.
My brother, your nose drew up air
and stopped it at the windpipe's node—
where are all those tricks now?

Broken is the thread, the sky fallen:
Where are all your words?
Day and night I am amazed;
no one explains. (Rest)

The world is still here,
but the body is not:
Gone is the philosopher.
The Joiner
lives in isolation—
who else is like Him?

Things cannot be joined,
they cannot be separated
if they are not first destroyed.
So who ever has a master?
Who, a servant?
Who goes to whom?

Kabir, say,
"My thoughts are turning
to that place where He dwells,
day and night.
Only He really knows His secret—
for He is beyond destruction."

From Raga Gauri

53

Meditation and worship
are my earrings,
true concepts, my beggar's blanket.
In the silent cave,
I sit in a yogic posture;
forsaking the world is my sect.

My King, I am the yogi of love;
I grieve neither at death nor separation. (Rest)

I blow my conch
in all the regions of the world;
this burning world is my ash-pouch.
Up-ending triple Maya is my yogic posture;
therefore I am saved,
though I am a householder.

I have made heart and breath
my two lyre-gourds,
aeons are this lyre's neck.
Its durable strings
never break.
This lyre plays without being touched.

Hearing it, my heart
becomes intoxicated:
I am not touched by surging Maya.
Kabir, say, "The ascetic
who plays this game
will not be born again."

54

Nine yards, ten yards, twenty-one yards
make one complete warp.
Sixty threads to a warp,
nine joinings, seventy-two crossthreads—
these being extra weft.

And so the soul went to have a body woven;
the weaver left his house. (Rest)

You can't measure it by yards,
or weigh it with measures,
though it needs five pounds of tempering.
If this tempering isn't available right away,
then there is an uproar in the house.

You are here for a few days only,
rebelling against the Master;
this moment won't return.
Gone are the clay-pots, the wetted bobbins—
the weaver left, frustrated.

You can't unwind thread from an empty bobbin;
the cloth-beam is no longer entangled.
Fool, get rid of all this confusion—leave it where it is—
this is what Kabir says in order to explain.

55

If light blends with light,
can it again be separated?
Those hearts empty of His name
burst and die.

My tawny, beautiful Ram,
my heart is devoted to you. (Rest)

By meeting a saint you gain perfection—
what use is yoga and sensual pleasure—

when you two meet all things are worked out
because you blend with Ram's name.

People think that this is merely a song—
it is a meditation on Brahma;
as in Benares, men hear Shiva's saving word
at the time of their death.

Whoever sings or hears
Hari's name intently,
Kabir, say, "There is no doubt
that person will reach the supreme stage."

56

So many tried,
but still they drowned:
They could not swim across
the world's ocean,
O my brother.
They observed rituals, duties,
adhered to vows,
yet still pride
burned away their hearts,
O my brother.

Why have you forgotten Thakur,
who is the giver of life and breath,
O my brother.
Birth is a precious diamond, a ruby,
yet you lost it for a cowrie,
O my brother. (Rest)

Thirst, yearning,
and the hunger of superstition
have touched you,
yet still you did not
place the guru's word
inside your soul,
O my brother.

Greedy for pleasure
you were driven
by carnal lusts:
You relished in the intoxication of evil,
O my brother.
Those who associate with sages,
through past good deeds,
are like iron
that floats with wood,
O my brother.

I am tired of wandering
from birth to birth.
I am weary
of sorrow's burden,
O my brother.

Kabir, say,
"Upon meeting the guru
you obtain supreme pleasure:
Love and devotion
will bear you across,
O my brother."

57

Like the paper cow elephant,
O my foolish heart,
such is Jagdish's sport.
Driven by lust,
the bull elephant is caught,
O my foolish heart,
and it has to suffer the goad.

Keep away from evil,
be absorbed in Hari:
Learn to understand,
O my foolish heart.
You never praised Hari fearlessly,
O my foolish heart,
nor did you board Ram's ship. (Rest)

For a fistful of grain, a monkey,
O my foolish heart
spreads out its hand;
frightened, it tries to escape—
still it dances,
O my foolish heart,
before every home.

Like the naive parrot
caught by a snare,
O my foolish heart,
such is Maya's way.
Like the evanescent color of a safflower,
O my foolish heart,
such is this world's expanse.

The world's thick with holy places
where you can bathe,
O my foolish heart,
and there are so many gods
you can worship.
Kabir, say, "They cannot free you,
O my foolish heart,
only slavery to Hari makes you free."

58

Fire can't burn it,
wind can't blow it away,
thieves can't come near it:
Gather the wealth
of Ram's name—
it can never be used up.

My wealth is Madho, Gobind, Dharnidhar:
He is the best of wealths.
The peace found
in Prabhu Gobind's service
cannot be matched,
though you become a high king. (Rest)

Shiva with Brahma's four sons
searched for this wealth,
having forsaken the world.
If Mukanda is in your heart,
Narayana on your tongue,
then Yama's noose can't ensnare you.

The heart of a great man
is absorbed in the pure abundance
of knowledge and devotion, given by the guru.
It is like water to the burning,
like a pillar for the tottering mind:
The fetters of superstition break.

Kabir says, "You, who are drunk with lust,
should examine your hearts and think:
In your houses you have
hundreds and thousands
of horses and elephants—
but in my house I have only Murari."

59

Like a monkey holding
a fistful of peas
who won't let go
because of greed,
so all your deeds,
done for greed,
will hang around your neck.

You lived your life uselessly.
Without devotion,
without the friendship of sages,
without worshipping Bhagwan,
truth can nowhere be found. (Rest)

Like a safflower
blossoming in the wild,
whose fragrance none can enjoy,

so one wanders
through many births,
cut down again and again
by death.

All this wealth,
youth, sons, wife,
given to you to enjoy,
caught and entangled you:
All the lusts
ensnared you
and pulled you down.

Life's fire,
the body's straw-house —
it's the same everywhere.
Kabir, say, "In order to swim across
this horrid world's ocean,
I held on to the True Guru
for my support."

60

Dirty water,
white earth:
From these
a puppet was formed.

I am nothing. Nothing is mine.
Body, wealth, life, O Gobind, are Yours. (Rest)

Breath was blended
with this earth;
the puppet began to walk,
infused with false delusion.

Many saved and amassed
hundreds of thousands —
but in the end
the clay-pot shattered.

Kabir, say, "The sole foundation
that you laid
was destroyed in a minute,
O proud one."

61

Praise Ram, O my soul,
like this, like this—
just as Dhruva and Prahlada
worshipped Hari.

O Dindayal, my hope is in You:
My entire family has boarded the raft. (Rest)

If it is Your will,
Your order will be obeyed,
and this raft will cross over
to the other side.

By the guru's grace
I have been enlightened;
gone forever
is my coming and going.

Kabir, say,
"Praise Sarangpani;
recognize Him as the only one
in this world and the next."

62

When you came into the world,
forsaking the womb,
you forgot the Master,
as soon as air touched you.

O my soul,
sing Hari's praise. (Rest)

While you did penance in the womb,
hanging upside down,
you were safe
from the womb's fire.

You returned, after wandering
through eight hundred and forty thousand lives;
if you miss out now,
there won't be any place for you.

Kabir, say,
"Praise Sarangpani,
who has never come here
nor is known to have gone away."

From Raga Gauri-Purabi

63

Do not yearn for heaven,
nor fear burning in hell;
what is to happen will happen—
do not have hopes in your heart.

Sing the praises of beautiful Ram
from whom we can obtain the supreme treasure. (Rest)

What use is worship, penance, purity,
fasting, and bathing at holy places,
if we do not know how to love
and devote ourselves to Bhagwan.

Do not rejoice upon seeing good fortune,
nor weep upon seeing misfortune.
Good fortune is the same as misfortune:
What He contrives comes to pass.

Kabir, say, "I know now
He lives in the hearts of saints.
That servant serves well
in whose heart dwells Murari."

From Raga Gauri

64

O my heart, you have no one—
why drag the weight of others.
As a tree is home to birds,
so is this world.

I have drunk Ram's ambrosia,
O my brother,
and it has made me forget
all other ambrosias. (Rest)

Why weep when others die?—
we too will not live forever.
That which is born must die.
Why should we cry with sorrow?

Life is absorbed from whence it sprang—
so drink with all the sages.
Kabir, say, "This is what I think:
Remember Ram, forsake all else."

65

A loving wife
looks at the road
with tear-filled eyes, and sighs.
Her heart cannot be appeased,
her feet do not move—
she hopes to see her lord.

"Fly, fly away, O black raven,
so that I may meet my dear Ram quickly." (Rest)

Kabir, say,
"To receive true life,
devote yourself to Hari.
Narayana's name is a pillar;
let your tongue say 'Ram.' "

66

All around were thick basil bushes,
and He was singing sweetly in the forest,
O my friend.
Seeing His beauty, the milkmaid was enthralled:
"Don't go away,
leaving me all alone,
O my beloved."

My heart touches Your feet,
O Sarangdhar—
only the most lucky
can meet You. (Rest)

In Bindraban, the alluring, the heart-enticing
Krishna grazed His cows,
O my friend.
He, whose only master is You,
O Sarangdhar—
his name is Kabir,
O my beloved.

From Raga Gauri-Purabi

67

Many wear flowing robes —
what good is living in forests?
What good is incense to gods,
O my brother?
Why dip in holy pools?

O my soul, I know you must go —
O child, understand the Invisible.
What I see will never be the same again:
All are in Maya's embrace. (Rest)

Wisemen, thinkers, great teachers,
all are caught in this world's net.
Kabir, say,
"Without the name of the one Ram,
this world is blind in Maya."

From Raga Gauri

68

O heart,
put away doubt
and dance fearlessly:
All this is Maya's artifice.
Does a bold warrior fear the battlefield?
Does a suttee worry about pots and pans?

Quit faltering,
O my foolish heart:
The vermilion-filled coconut
is in your hand —
now you must burn and receive renown. (Rest)

The world is destroyed
because it is busy
with lust, wrath, Maya.
Kabir, say,
"Forsake not Raja Ram,
who is the highest of the high."

69

Your command is ever before me —
how can I go against it?
You are the river, You the boatman,
You Yourself will bear me across.

Friend, take up His praise,
though the Master be wrathful or loving. (Rest)

Your name is my pillar,
like a flower blooming in water.
Kabir, say, "I am His house-slave;
He can keep me or kill me."

70

After wandering through
eight hundred and forty thousand lives,
Nanda grew weary, O my brother.
Then God became incarnate,
because of his devotion —
great was that poor man's luck,
O my brother.

Tell me, you who say
that He became Nanda's son,
whose son was Nanda?
When there was no earth, sky,
nor this entire world,
where was this Nanda then,
O my brother? (Rest)

He who is beyond affliction,
beyond birth,
His name is Niranjan,
O my brother.
Kabir's swami is that Lord
who has neither mother nor father,
O my brother.

71

Malignantly, malignantly,
people malign me.
Actually, malice befits servants.
Malice is my father,
malice is my mother. (Rest)

If I am maligned
I shall go to heaven,

hoarding the Name's treasure
in my heart.
If I am maligned,
I am purified:
maligners wash my clothes.

He who maligns me
is my friend;
my heart
is inside each maligner.
The real maligner is he
who stops his malice.
Maligners wish me a long life.

Malice is my love
and affection;
malice saves me.
For the slave Kabir,
malice is the best treasure —
maligners drown,
while I swim across.

72

Ram, Ram, so fearless are You
that You Yourself became the raft
in order to save us. (Rest)

When I exist
You do not;
now You exist
and I do not.
Now You and I are one:
Seeing us unite,
my heart is filled with pleasure.

When I have wisdom
I have no strength;
now I have neither wisdom
nor strength.

Kabir, say,
"My wisdom was snatched away
and transformed—
and I was perfected."

73

From the six spheres,
a little house was made
in which was placed a thing unique.
Breath became its lock and key;
it didn't take long to make.

Keep your heart awake now,
O my brother.
You've already lost your life
because of neglect—
thieves entered and robbed your house. (Rest)

Five watchmen stood at the door,
but they could not be trusted.
Be alert and think clearly,
and take in the light
that will cleanse you.

When the beautiful woman
saw the nine houses,
she forgot that thing unique.
Kabir, say, "When the nine houses were robbed,
that which was forgotten went to dwell in the tenth."

74

O my mother,
I never knew anyone else:
Only He abides in my heart,
whose virtues Shiva
and Brahma's four sons sang. (Rest)

My heart was enlightened
when the guru

granted me understanding:
My thoughts reached the sky's sphere.
Gone were sin, defect, fear, fetters —
in my heart's house
I knew solace.

My soul's love was blended with the One:
I have realized and recognized Prabhu —
my heart thinks of no one else.
I have abandoned all other desires:
I am infused
with sandalwood perfume.
Gone is all my pride.

Prabhu's abiding place
is in her
who sings and ponders
the Master's glory.
Fortunate is she
in whose heart He lives:
Great is her destiny.

When Maya was cut off,
Shiva's wisdom shone through:
I blended with the One.
Kabir, say, "Upon meeting the guru,
I found great solace —
my wandering is over.
Happy is my heart."

The Acrostic of Kabir

From Raga Gauri-Purabi

1

The three worlds are in these fifty-two letters:
All things are in them.
These letters will pass away—
but the letter for Him is not among these.

2

Where there are words, you need letters;
where there are no words, the mind ceases to be.
He is present with or without words:
None can describe His reality.

3

If I find the Unfindable, what will I say?
And if I do speak—to what end?
As the banyan tree is blended with the seed,
so He pervades the three worlds.

4

While searching for the Unsearchable,
I guessed the secret and understood a little.
The secret turned and pierced my heart,
and I found the Imperishable, the Unknowable.

5

Turks know the precepts,
Hindus, the Vedas and the Puranas.
Some knowledge should be read
to make the mind understand.

6

I know Omkar, the Primal:
I don't trust what can be written or said.
Those who understand Omkar
will never be erased.

7

K.   Once sunrays have fallen on a lotus,
     it will not again close in moonlight.
     And if I picked out that lotus's essence,
     how would I describe it?

8

KH. My heart enters a hollowed tree-trunk;
     it doesn't fly about, leaving this hollow.
     Seeing the Master, it dwells with Khimakar.
     Receiving the Indelible, it becomes indelible.

9

G.   The guru's words — those who know them
     turn their eyes to nothing else.
     They are like birds, which have never flown off;
     grasping the Unseizable they flit away into the sky.

10

GH. He is present in every pore;
     if a clay-pot shatters, He does not diminish.
     The raft is in your own heart:
     Leaving the ferryman, you ran off to the ravines.

11

NG. Hold on to love, let go of doubt.
     Don't run away
     when you encounter difficulty:
     This is the highest of wisdoms.

12

CH. Creation is a huge painting —
    forget this painting; think of the Painter.
    This painting is beautiful — that's the problem:
    Forget the painting; think of the Painter.

13

CHH. Why don't you live with Chhatrapati?
    Be strong. Forsake all other hopes.
    O my heart, each moment I tell you,
    if you leave Him, you will be ensnared.

14

J. Those who burn body, youth, vigor, while living
    shall find the way. Those who burn to ash
    all external and internal desires
    shall find the light of wisdom.

15

JH. You knew only traps, never escape;
    you always hesitated and were never accepted.
    Why are you wasting time advising others?
    You knew only quarrels — and that's what you got.

16

NY. He is very near — right in your own heart.
    Why do you leave Him and wander far away?
    He for whom you searched the world over
    is so very near.

17

T. Unwieldy is the raft that's in the heart.
    Why don't you open the doors and enter the palace?
    Behold the Immoveable — you need go nowhere else.
    Embrace Him, and your heart will find love.

18

TH.   She is like water in a mirage—
       I looked carefully and my heart grew calm.
       The deceiver that devoured the whole world
       I myself robbed—calm now is my heart.

19

D.   When you fear, you become fearless:
       All other fears merge with that fear.
       If you fear that fear, then you will be fearful—
       be fearless, and all your fears will flee.

20

DH.   Search nearby—why go so far?
       Your soul wearied in the long search.
       You even climbed Mount Sumeru. When you returned,
       you found Him in your own house.

21

N.   The man who conquers on the battlefield,
       who does not bend or surrender,
       is thought most fortunate in life:
       He kills the leader and lets all others go.

22

T.   You cannot ford the unfordable;
       so the body keeps embracing the world.
       When the three worlds blend with your body,
       your soul blends with His, and you find truth.

23

TH.   You cannot fathom the fathomless.
       He is unfathomable—all this here is transient.
       On a single plot of land you build a city,
       and without pillars you support a house.

24

D. All that you see will pass away:
   Keep the Invisible in your heart.
   When you fit the key to the tenth door,
   you will behold Dayal.

25

DH. When the High rules the low,
    the low abide with the High:
    They leave the bottom and go to the heights;
    uniting with the High, they find peace.

26

N. Day and night she spent looking and waiting:
   Expectant eyes mad with desire.
   When she sees Him, after waiting so long,
   the watcher and the Watched will unite.

27

P. The Endless has no end:
   I am in love with the Supreme Light.
   I overcame the five senses—
   now I am beyond sin and virtue.

28

PH. Fruit without flower:
    Take a small slice and escape
    that gorge. Pore over this slice:
    It peels away the body.

29

B. Drop mixes with waterdrop,
   and the two cannot be separated.
   Become His slave—serve Him in love;
   become a bard and discover your fetters.

30

BH.   Secret blends with secret:
       Fear is smashed and hope gained.
       He who is outside is also inside:
       I know the secret and have seen Bhupati.

31

M.   Get at the root and quench your heart:
       Know your soul through this secret.
       Why hesitate to blend your soul:
       Be ecstatic and find truth.

32

M.   My interest is in the mind—
       by disciplining the mind you become enlightened.
       To the mind, to the mind, say, O Kabir,
       "O mind, I have found none like you."

33

The mind is Shakti; the mind is Shiva;
the mind animates the five senses.
Overcome the mind and be intoxicated
and so speak about the three worlds.

34

Y.   If you want to understand, then destroy
       evil thoughts, subjugate the city of the body.
       Stay on the battlefield, and do not flee—
       only then will you be called a hero.

35

R.   Consider taste as without taste:
       Being unable to taste will lead to tasting.
       Leave this taste and find that Taste.
       Acquire that Taste and this one turns distasteful.

36

L. Place unfading love in your heart,
    which leads to supreme truth.
    Tie your heart with love's string
    and find the Unfindable and dwell at His feet.

37

V. Remember Vishnu, again and again:
    Remembering Vishnu never leads to defeat.
    I serve Vishnu's sons, who sing His praises.
    Upon meeting Vishnu, truth is secured.

38

VA. Know Him. By knowing Him,
     you become like Him.
     When this and That blend together
     none can tell them apart.

39

S. Stash Him away carefully.
    Forget about satisfying your body.
    Your body will be satisfied when you love,
    when the Raja of the three worlds permeates it.

40

KH. If you begin to search for Him
     and find Him — you will not return.
     If you search, find, and contemplate, you won't
     take long to swim across this horrid water.

41

SH. She who graces her husband's bed,
     truly banishes doubt.
     She forsakes petty pleasures for the supreme one:
     Only then is she called a wife, and he, a husband.

42

H.   He exists—yet you knew Him not.
      Knowledge of Him will gratify you.
      He exists, as understand those who can.
      Then there's only Him, and not all this.

43

Everyone says, "I want, I want."
Hence all this sorrow.
But if you fall in love with Lakshmi's husband,
sorrow is banished and solace found.

44

KH.   Many perished. Countless perish still:
      They never had Him in their thoughts.
      Restrain your heart; see the world's reality:
      Merge with, from whence you separated.

45

Many have joined these fifty-two letters;
none saw the one Letter.
O Kabir, those who speak the word of truth
are real pundits, who live fearlessly.
Joining letters may be the business of pundits,
but thinking of truth is the business of the wise.
A person's wisdom is proportional to his mind,
Kabir, say, "He can understand only that much."

Kabir's Lunar Days

From Raga Gauri

Sloka

Fifteen lunar days; seven weekdays.
Kabir, say, "They have neither a bank on this side,
nor a bank on that side."
Sages and saints learn the secret:
The Creator, Deva, is everywhere.

I

On the moonless day, give up longing.
Remember Ram who knows our innermost thoughts.
While living, find salvation's door:
Perceive the real Word and Source of all things.

When you love Gobind's lotus-like feet,
your heart becomes pure, by the grace of saints.
Stay awake day and night
and sing Hari's praise. (Rest)

1

At the new moon, think of the Beloved;
the Formless, the Endless one, sports in each heart.
Death will not eat your body,
if you remain absorbed in the First Being.

2

The second day: Perceive the body's two parts:
Maya and Brahma are blended in all things.
He neither increases nor diminishes;
He is casteless, formless, the same forever.

3

The third day: Blend the three qualities,
and find the supreme one, the source of bliss.
There is hope in the company of sages—
there is light both within and without.

4

The fourth day: Rein in your restive heart;
do not lust or harbor anger.
He is present in water and in earth:
Blend into His presence and sing His praise.

5

The fifth day: Five elements scattered everywhere:
The world is busy chasing gold and women.
Drink love's pure ambrosia
and you shall never grow old and die.

6

The sixth day: The six spheres wander off;
without love they cannot stand still.
Put away doubt and be patient:
Don't bother with religious rituals.

7

The seventh day: Remember the Word is true.
Thread Ram in your heart;
be free from fear and rub off pain—
find solace in the silent pool.

8

The eighth day: Remember the body has eight elements
where the nameless Treasure is stored.
A great guru can reveal the secret:
Turn towards the deathless, unmoving One.

9

The ninth day: Guard the nine doors
and stem the flow of desire.
Abandon greed and worldly love
and live forever, eating the immortal fruit.

10

The tenth day: Bliss is everywhere.
Gone is doubt. Gobind is found:
The matchless, the beautiful Light,
flawless, without malice, without shade or sunshine.

11

The eleventh day: Walk the way
and you will not suffer rebirth—
your body will be serene, pure.
He is near who was said to be far away.

12

The twelfth day: Twelve suns rise;
trumpets unblown sound day and night.
You shall see the Father of the three worlds.
Here's the miracle: From the man emerges Shiva.

13

The thirteenth day: Sing of the hidden One.
He is the same, both above and below;
He is neither high nor low, august nor base:
Ram is diffused equally throughout.

14

The fourteenth day: He is everywhere;
Murari is present in every pore.
Contemplate patience and truth;
tell the story of Brahma's wisdom.

II

The full moon fills the sky,
unfurling all its sixteen parts.
Beginning, middle, end: He is steadfast.
Kabir is soaked in the sea of solace.

Kabir's Days of the Week

From Raga Gauri

I

Day by day sing Hari's praises.
Go to your guru and find His secret.

1

Sunday launches devotion.
Bridle desires in your body's temple,
and you will be fragrant day and night;
untouched, flutes will play softly in your heart.

2

Monday makes ambrosia drip from the moon:
Taste it and vitiate poison.
Dwell at His door, leashed by the Word—
let your drunk heart drink.

3

Tuesday builds a fort;
know the ways of the five thieves.
Don't leave this fort and go away—
the raja might meet with misfortune.

4

Wednesday enlightens the mind:
in your heart's lotus, Hari takes up abode;
the guru ties the two together,
straightening out the bent petals.

5

Thursday drowns Maya
and brings together the three gods.
You cannot wash away the sins of many days
where the three rivers meet.

6

Friday props you with good deeds;
you climb higher and fight against self
day and night. It restrains the five senses,
so that you may not see falsely.

7

Saturday carefully guards the flame
of the heart's little lamp;
you are illumined inside out,
and all your past doings will be as nothing.

II

When you are worrying about other things,
how can you enter His palace?
Learn to love Ram by praising Him.
Say, Kabir, "Only then will your body be pure."

From Raga Asa

1

Touching my guru's feet I ask,
why is the soul created?
Why is it made and then destroyed?
Speak, so that I may understand.

O holy one, have mercy; show me the path
where fear's fetters break.
Birth, death are full of sorrow:
Escape from rebirth is solace. (Rest)

If the soul does not break Maya's fetters,
it cannot blend into Silence.
If it does not see salvation's true source,
it cannot be free from fear.

The soul is not born as you think:
It is free from being and nonbeing;
cease thinking about waxing and waning—
be absorbed into eternal, constant love.

As a reflection in water blends
with the water-pot when it shatters,
Kabir, say, "So, through virtue, doubts flee
and the soul is absorbed into Silence."

2

Three-and-a-half-yard gowns,
thick holy threads,
rosaries on their necks,

gleaming vessels in their hands—
don't call them Hari's saints—
rather the thugs of Benares.

Saints like these
I can do without—
they devour both the tree
and its branches. (Rest)

They place scrubbed pots
on a fire
of washed wood;
they dig up the earth
to make two fresh hearths daily—
and they gobble up all of mankind.

These sinners
wander in guilt,
saying they are *aparas* yogis.
They strut about
filled with pride—
while their own families drown.

You have to stay where you're put:
And your deeds
reflect your position.
Kabir, say,
"Those who meet the True Guru
will never again be reborn."

3

My Father comforted me,
put nectar in my mouth
and laid me
on a soft bed.
Why should I
take Him out of my heart?
When I leave,
I won't lose.

My mother died—and I'm happy.
Though shirtless, I'm not cold. (Rest)

I can forfeit my life
for my Father who begot me.
Those five
are my friends no longer:
I killed and crushed them underfoot.
My mind and body
are drenched.

My Father
is the great Gosain:
How can I
approach Him?
The true guru
showed me the way—
my soul is happy
with the world's Father.

I am Your son,
You are my Father:
two abodes
in one place.
Kabir says,
"The servant has found Him out—
I have solved the riddle,
by the guru's grace."

4

A dressed chicken in one pot,
wine in another.
All around sit five yogis,
with the noseless queen in the middle.

Clang, clang rings the queen's bell—
the wise have broken away from you, O queen. (Rest)

The noseless queen dwells in everyone;
killing all, she looks for more.

She says, "I am everyone's sister or niece;
I am the slave of any man who marries me.

"Wise is my husband—
he calls himself a saint;
only he stands over me—
others can't come near."

Her nose, her ears were cut;
she was thrown out, beaten and mutilated.
Kabir says, "She is the enemy of saints—
and the beloved of the entire world."

5

Yogis, ascetics, hermits, mendicants,
and all those who roam in pilgrimage,
those who wear ropes
and pluck, shave, or mat their hair—
all in the end must die.

Then why not worship Ram?
What can Yama do, if your tongue loves Ram? (Rest)

Those who know the Shastras,
the Vedas, astronomy,
and all that grammar;
those who know spells, mantras, medicine—
all in the end must die.

Those who revel in empires, canopied thrones,
countless alluring women,
betel, camphor,
and sandalwood's sweet fragrance—
all in the end must die.

I have searched all the Vedas,
the Puranas, the Smriti—
salvation lies in none.
Kabir says, "So I repeat Ram's name—
he erases birth and rebirth."

6

An elephant plays a rebeck,
the ox, a drum,
and a raven clangs the cymbals.
The donkey dances, wearing a robe,
and the buffalo becomes a saint.

Raja Ram, bitter *akk*-pods become ripe mangoes—
few can solve the riddle and eat them. (Rest)

Sitting in his house,
a lion prepares betel
with the folded betel-leaves a mole brings.
In every house, mice sing of bliss,
and a turtle blows the conch.

The motherless son gets married:
Canopies of gold are erected.
He marries a most beautiful woman;
the hare sings
the lion's praises.

Kabir says, "Listen, O saints:
an ant eats a mountain;
the turtle says,
'I need fire,'
and a gnat recites the Word."

7

One bag, seventy-two pockets—
but only one opening:
Those who beg
across this wide earth
are the world's greatest yogis.

Only they will find the nine treasures
who drive their souls up to graze in the sky. (Rest)

Wisdom's blanket, meditation's needle:
Twist the Word's thread
and put it through the needle's eye.
The five elements are your deerskin:
In this way walk on the Guru's path.

Mercy's shovel, body's pile of chaff:
Set it alight with the fire of understanding.
When His love is inside you,
you will sit enraptured
throughout the four ages.

All yoga is Ram's name,
who gives body and breath.
Kabir, say, "If He is merciful,
He will give you
His true sign."

<h1 style="text-align:center">8</h1>

Where have Hindus and Turks come from?
Who started
these fine distinctions?
Think, ponder in your heart, fool:
Who will go to heaven or hell?

Hey qazi, what book are you expounding now?
Others like you read, thought, and died—
none ever got the message. (Rest)

For love of woman
you circumcise—
I shall never believe, O my brother.
If Khuda had wanted me to be a Turk—
He would have cut it off himself.

If circumcision makes you a Turk—
what are you going to do with women.
Since you haven't given up woman,
who is half your body,
you are really a Hindu.

Put away that book
and praise Ram, fool—
you are carrying out great cruelty.
Kabir has taken hold of Ram:
Turks live on in misery.

9

As long as a lamp has oil and wick,
all things are visible.
When the oil is used up,
the wick flickers and goes out,
and the house becomes desolate.

Fool, no one will keep you for a minute;
so repeat Ram's name. (Rest)

Who really has a mother?
Tell me, who really has a father?
When your body bursts, none remembers you—
there's only, "Get him out, get him out."

Your mother sits weeping
on the threshold;
your brother makes off with the bed.
With dishevelled hair, your wife weeps:
The swan must fly alone.

Kabir says, "Hear, O saints,
about this horrid ocean:
Man must suffer cruelty;
and Yama never goes away,
O honored saints."

10

Sanaka and Sanandana never found the end;
Brahma wasted away his life reading the Vedas.

Churn Hari's churn gently, O my brother,
so you won't lose the butter. (Rest)

Make your body your churn, mind your churning-stick,
and pour in the Word's rennet.

Make the mind's meditation Hari's churn,
and by the guru's grace find the ambrosia's source.

Kabir, say, "If the King is merciful, you will hold on
to Ram's name and alight on the far shore."

11

The oil is gone, the wick dry;
silent is the drum, the dancer sleeps.

The fire is out; there is no smoke—
He is everywhere; there is no one else. (Rest)

Broken is the string, the rebeck silent:
Carelessness has ruined many things.

Sermons, scoldings, sayings, stories—
all are forgotten: You have gained insight.

Kabir says, "Those who shatter the five senses
are not far from supreme bliss."

12

Although a son makes many mistakes,
his mother remembers none of them.

O my precious Ram, I am your child—
why do you not forget my mistakes? (Rest)

Although a son hits his mother in wrath,
even then she remembers nothing.

My heart is lost in the labyrinth of sorrow;
how can I get out without His name?

Give my heart purity of wisdom,
and softly, softly Kabir will sing Your praise.

13

Hajj for me is going to the Gomti's banks
where dwells the Pitambar Pir.

Beautiful, beautiful. How sweetly He sings,
arousing ardor in my heart for Hari's name. (Rest)

Narada and Sharda wait on Him;
nearby sits lady Kamla, His handmaid.

With a rosary on my neck, "Ram" on my tongue,
I offer Him my salaam, uttering His myriad names.

Kabir says, "Sing Ram's praises
so that both Hindus and Turks may understand."

14

Gardener's girl
gathering petals,
don't you know
each petal has life.
The stone
for which you pluck these petals
is lifeless.

Gardener's girl you have forgotten,
the True Guru is the living Deva. (Rest)

Brahma is in petals,
Vishnu in branches,
and Shankara Deva in flowers —
right before my eyes
you have broken
three gods —
whom do you worship?

The idol was made
by chiselling stone;
often the sculptor
put his foot on its chest.
If this idol were real,
it would have devoured
the sculptor.

Rice, lentils,
flour pudding,
crispy *kasar*
are all eaten
by the priests,
who leave only ashes
for the idol.

Gardener's girl
you have forgotten,
the world
has forgotten—
but I have not forgotten:
Kabir, say, "Ram looks after me;
merciful is Hari Rai."

15

You were a child
up to twelve.
But even at twenty,
you did no penance.
By your thirtieth year
you worshipped no god—
now you are full of regret
in your old age.

Life passed you by;
you were busy saying, "Mine, mine."
The ocean has dried up,
your arms have withered. (Rest)

You built a wall
around a dried-up pool;
you fenced off
a harvested field.
The thief came
and made off
with all that you were trying
to make your own, O fool.

Your head, hands,
and feet quiver;
endlessly rheum flows
from your eyes;
your tongue can't say one word
without stuttering—
why now do you want to do
pious deeds?

If Hari is merciful
He will place love in your heart,
and you shall obtain
the fruit of His name.
By the guru's grace
you will find Hari's treasure,
which will go with you
even in the end.

Kabir says,
"Listen, O saints,
you cannot take food
or wealth with you.
When the call comes from Gopal Rai
you have to go, leaving wealth and home."

16

Some have silk clothes,
some beds of silk;
some have straw shacks,
some not even a tattered blanket.

O my heart, do not complain and grumble;
receive all things with thanks, O my heart. (Rest)

The clay that the potter kneads is all the same;
he only paints it with different colors:
some are filled with pearls and precious jewels,
others are filled with filth.

The miser is given wealth to keep,
but the fool calls it his very own.
When Yama's staff hits him on the pate
things are settled quite quickly.

Hari's slaves are called the highest saints:
They find solace in obeying His decree.
Truth for them is what pleases Him,
and they place His will in their hearts.

Kabir says, "Listen, O saints,
saying, 'Mine, mine' is wrong.
Broken is the cage, the bird taken—
the seed and water-bowl are all that is left."

17

I am a poor man of God.
You like to rule over people.
Allah the Primal, the Master of religions,
never ordained cruelty.

Hey, qazi,
your words don't suit you. (Rest)

Fasting, praying, and saying the creed
will never get you to heaven.
The Ka'aba is right inside your heart—
if you really want to know.

Those doing justice in reality pray—
their creed is recognizing Him through wisdom;

their prayer-rugs blind the senses.
In this way they realize true religion.

Discern the Master, be merciful;
root out pride—make it blunt.
Look upon others as you look upon yourself—
only then will you join the heavenly host.

The clay is the same, many the disguises:
Recognize Brahma in everyone.
Kabir says, "You have forsaken heaven
and satisfied yourself with hell."

18

Not a drop falls from the sky on your city.
Where has all the music gone?
Parbrahma, Parmeshwar, Madho,
the Primal Soul has taken it away.

O my brother, where are your words,
which were always a part of you—
the stories, the speeches, the sayings
that danced in your head? (Rest)

Where is the musician
who played this drum?
Tales, words no longer flow out from you:
Your strength has been wrenched out.

Your once eager ears
are now completely deaf.
The strength of all your lusts
now has flagged.

Your feet are useless,
your hands limp;
not a word
escapes your mouth.

Weary are the five enemies, robbers all,
from their aimless wandering.
Your heart, your elephant-like mind are weary—
all these were once brisk, full of vigor.

Dead and gone are all your senses,
and your friends and brothers have left you.
Kabir says, "Those who remember Hari
break their bonds while still alive."

19

Nothing is stronger
than that she-snake
who tricked Brahma,
Vishnu, and Mahadeva.

Routing everyone,
she lives in a holy pool.
By the guru's grace, you can see her
who has strung together the three worlds. (Rest)

My brothers, why
do you shout, "Snake, snake";
those how know the True One
can easily kill her.

No one is safe from her sting.
But if you win over her,
even poor Yama
can't do anything about it.

She too is His creation;
winning or losing is beyond her control.
If she is around, you'll be reborn.
The guru's grace ferried Kabir across.

20

Why read the Smriti to a dog?
Why sing Hari's praise to a non-believer?

Remember Ram, Ram, Ram, always;
do not associate with non-believers. (Rest)

Why feed camphor to a crow?
Why give milk to a snake?

Sages will enlighten you:
The touchstone turns iron into gold.

A dog and a non-believer act as they must —
past deeds determine present actions.

If you watered a margosa with ambrosia,
Kabir says, "It would still be bitter."

21

Lanka for a castle,
the ocean for a moat —
still nothing remains
of Ravana's household.

What shall I ask for? Nothing endures.
My eyes see the world pass away. (Rest)

A hundred thousand sons,
a hundred and twenty thousand grandsons:
Now not even a lamp
or a wick in Ravana's house.

The moon and the sun
heated his kitchen,
fire came
and washed his clothes.

If, by the guru's guidance,
Ram's name is inside you,
you shall never wander from birth to birth;
you shall become steadfast.

Kabir says,
"Listen, O people,
there is no salvation
without Ram's name."

22

First comes the son, then the mother;
the guru touches his disciple's feet.

Listen to these marvels, my brothers:
I see a lion taking cattle out to graze. (Rest)

A fish lays eggs on top of a tree;
a cat carries off a dog.

A tree with branches below, roots above
bears flowers and fruit on its trunk.

A buffalo goes to graze, riding a horse;
an ox goes away and his load comes home.

Kabir says, "Those who want to solve the riddle
will know all if they repeat 'Ram.' "

23

From seed, He made your body,
and preserved it in the pit of fire:
He kept it for ten months in the womb.
When you emerged, Maya tainted you.

O mortal, why did you become greedy
and lose the jewel of life?
In past lives, why did you not
sow the seed in the earth? (Rest)

A child once — but now you are old:
What was to happen has happened.
When Yama came and grabbed you by the hair,
why did you then cry out?

You yearn for life:
Yama watches your every breath.
The world is a gamble, O Kabir,
cast your dice with care.

24

My body is a dye-tub:
I will dye my heart with purity.
The five virtues
will be my wedding guests,
and I will walk
around the fire with Ram Rai,
my soul suffused with His color.

Sing, sing, O maidens, songs of marriage:
Ram, my husband, has come to my house. (Rest)

In the lotus of my breath
I have planted the marriage canopy;
divine wisdom
is my marriage mantra.
Ram Rai has become
my husband:
Great has been my luck.

Wise men, saints, and ascetics
came to my marriage
in three million
three hundred thousand chariots.
Kabir says, "The one divine Bhagwan
has taken me away in marriage."

25

O my brother,
my mother-in-law hates me,
my father-in-law loves me,
and my eldest brother-in-law's very name
frightens me.

O my friends, my companions,
my sister-in-law has me in her claws.
My heart is aflame
because I am separated
from my youngest brother-in-law.

I am going mad: I have forgotten Ram.
How can I go on living, O my brother.
I have not seen Him
with my own eyes
who frolics with me in bed.

To whom can I tell my sorrow,
O my brother. (Rest)

My own body is my enemy.
Maya has made me mad.
While I was near my eldest brother,
I was cherished
by my husband.

Kabir says, "While struggling against
the five senses, I lost my life.
False Maya has ensnared the entire earth—
I found solace
by praising Ram."

26

In our house
we are forever
stretching out thread—
but around your neck
you have only one
sacrificial thread.
You read the Vedas
and recite the Gayatri,
while Gobind dwells
in our hearts.

On my tongue is Vishnu,
in my eyes Narayana,
in my heart Gobind.
When Mukanda questions you at Yama's door,
what will you say, O fool? (Rest)

We are cows, you are the cowherd,
O *gosain:*
our protector
from birth to birth.
But you never grazed us
on the far bank.
What kind of a master
do we have?

You are a Brahmin,
I, a weaver from Benares:
Can you guess
what I really mean?
While you were busy
begging from monarchs
and rajas,
my thoughts
were fixed
on Hari.

27

The world, life
are like dreaming:
Life is a dream.
I tied myself
to both life and world,
and abandoned
the eternal treasure.

Father, I have made love to Maya,
and she stole my jewel of wisdom. (Rest)

The moth perishes
even though it has eyes

to see:
The fool does not see fire.
Those in love
forget death's noose,
chasing gold and women.

Give heed,
forsake immorality,
and swim across.
Kabir, say, "Jagjivan is such
that there is none
like Him."

28

Though I have taken on
many forms
in the past,
I shall now take on none.
The lute's strings are slack:
I am in the power of Ram's name.

I no longer know how to dance:
My heart drums no longer. (Rest)

I have burned off
lust, anger, Maya;
greed's clay-pot
has shattered;
lust's robe is now threadbare:
Gone are all my doubts.

I now recognize
the One in all beings—
there's no need to quarrel.
Kabir, say,
"I have found God, the complete:
Ram has been merciful to me."

29

You fast,
trying to appease Allah;
you kill living beings
to appease your palate.
You do not see others
as you see yourself—
so what
are you raving about?

Hey, qazi, the Master is one:
He is yours—
and He is inside you.
Though you ponder and think,
you do not see Him.
Beguiled by religion,
you do not think:
Your life has gone to waste. (Rest)

Your holy books say
that Allah is true,
without whom
no man or woman can live.
O fool, reading is useless
if you fail
to understand
with your heart.

Allah is hidden
in each body—
think about it.
He is the same
both in Hindus and Turks:
This is what Kabir
is shouting out
so loudly.

30

I adorned myself for our tryst,
but Hari, Jagjivan, Gosain never came.

Hari is my husband;
I am Hari's bride.
Ram is great,
and I am a frail girl. (Rest)

Wife and husband live in one house;
they share one bed—but there is no union.

Blessed is the bride who pleases her Beloved.
Kabir, say, "She will not suffer rebirth."

31

Only a diamond
can pierce a diamond:
The heart,
capricious as the wind,
is absorbed
into the Constant.
A certain diamond
pierced all life—
this I learned
from my true guru.

Hari's praise is the eternal teaching:
Become a swan and see the diamond. (Rest)

Kabir, say,
"I have seen
that diamond
that is suffused
throughout this world.
This hidden diamond
becomes visible

when your wise guru
reveals it
to you."

32

My first wife was ugly, low-caste,
and evil in character,
both in her father's house
and in her father-in-law's house.
But my second wife is beautiful,
enlightened, and good-natured—
with great joy
I place her on my belly.

I am glad that my first wife died.
May you live long, O my new bride. (Rest)

Kabir, say,
"When this younger wife came,
the older one's fortune
abandoned her.
The younger
now lives with me—
the older
has gone elsewhere."

33

At first my wife was called Dhanya;
now they call her Ramjanya.

These baldheads have destroyed my house—
even my little son is saying, "Ram." (Rest)

Kabir says, "Listen, O my mother,
these baldheads have destroyed my caste."

34

Stop, stop, my young wife,
stop veiling your face—
in the end
you won't be worth a penny.

The one before you,
often veiled her face—
please don't adopt
her habits.

There's only one advantage
in veiling your face:
For a few days, people will say,
"Oh, they have a new daughter-in-law."

Your veil
would be fitting only
if you swayed and danced
and sang Hari's praise.

Kabir says,
"Only that bride will prevail
who spends her life
singing Hari's praise."

35

I would rather be sawed in half
than see You turn Your back to me.
Come, embrace me,
and listen to my plea.

I would sacrifice myself for You.
Come, turn Your face, my Beloved.
Look at me—
why are You torturing me? (Rest)

If You want to saw my limbs,
I will not flinch.

Even if You kill my body,
I will not stop loving You.

There is no difference
between You and me.
You are that same husband,
I that same wife.

Kabir says,
"Listen, O world;
Now I no longer
can have faith in you."

36

You know not the Weaver's secret,
who weaved this entire world. (Rest)

While you listened to the Vedas, the Puranas,
I was stretching out my warp.

He made looms of earth and sky;
the sun and moon were trellis rods.

He pressed the pedals and wove all this:
My heart has found that Weaver.

I, a weaver, have found Him in my own home:
I recognize Ram in all of life.

Kabir says, "I have smashed my loom;
now the Weaver joins thread with thread."

37

If you are dirty within,
and you bathe at shrines,
it won't get you to heaven.
Nothing is gained
by pleasing people:
Ram is no fool.

Worship Ram, the only Deva.
The Guru's service is the true ablution. (Rest)

If bathing in water
brings salvation —
then frogs are forever bathing.
And like these frogs
are such people:
Again and again they are reborn.

If a callous fool
dies in Benares,
he won't be saved from hell.
If a saint of Hari
dies in Haramba,
he can save a whole army.

Where day and night
exist not;
where there are no Vedas or Shastras —
there dwells Nirankar.
Kabir, say, "Meditate upon Him,
O fools of the world."

From Raga Gujari

1

Four hooves, two horns,
a mute mouth —
how then will you sing
His praise?
Whether you sit
or stand,
there will always be
a stick hitting you —
where are you going to hide
your head?

Without Hari,
you will be someone else's ox:
Your nose will be slit,
your shoulders broken,
and you will eat useless chaff. (Rest)

All day long,
you will stagger
in the forest —
and still
your stomach
will not be full.
But you never heeded
the advice of holy men:
You have gotten
what you've earned.

Pain and pleasure
will drown you
in delusion,

as you wander
through countless
births and rebirths.
Forgetting Prabhu,
you lost life's jewel—
when again
will you get this chance?

You will tread
round and round
like an ox
rotating an oil-seed mill,
or dance like some monkey;
your nights will be uneasy.
Kabir says,
"Without Ram's name,
you will beat your head
and wail."

2

With sobs and whimpers,
Kabir's mother weeps:
"How will these children live,
O Raghurai.

"Kabir has given up
setting the loom and weaving:
He has written Hari's name
on his body." (Rest)

"When I wind thread
on the bobbin,
I forget
my most dear Ram:

"I'm slow-witted,
and a weaver by caste—

but my profit
is Hari's name."

Kabir says,
"Listen, O my mother:
Raghurai is my provider—
and theirs as well."

From Raga Sorath

1

Hindus died worshipping idols,
Turks died bowing heads.
They burn, these bury—
neither learned Your reality.

O my heart, the world is deep darkness:
All are caught in Yama's noose. (Rest)

Poets died reading poetry,
kapris died going to Kedara.
Yogis died matting their long hair—
they too never learned Your reality.

Rajas died gathering wealth,
burying hoards of gold.
Pundits died reading the Vedas,
women died adorning their faces.

All are lost without Ram's name—
think about it in your heart:
Who has ever been saved without Ram's name?
That's what Kabir is really saying.

2

When the body burns
it becomes ash,
when stashed away,
an army of worms eats it up;
like water in an unfired clay-pot:
That is the body's only boast.

Why go about swollen with pride?
Have you forgotten those ten months
when you hung upside down? (Rest)

Like honey collected by a bee,
so a fool collects money
by hardship and thrift.
But when he dies, they say,
"Take, take him away.
Why keep a corpse for so long?"

His wife goes with him,
but only as far as the door;
after that friends carry him.
But family and friends
go only as far as the cremation ground—
after that the swan is all alone.

Kabir says,
"Listen, O mortals,
those who fell into death's well,
let themselves be tied
by false Maya,
like parrots attracted to the trap."

3

After listening
to the Vedas, the Puranas,
you are forced to put your trust
in rituals.
All the wise people
were seized by death;
even pundits left
with hopes unfulfilled.

O my heart, you neglected one thing:
You did not praise Raja Raghupati. (Rest)

Those who go to forests
to do penance and meditate,

gathering and eating all kinds of roots,
nadis, bedis, shabdis, munis —
all are on Yama's ledger.

They do not know
the path of love —
yet they draw circles and lines
on their bodies.
They deceive
by singing ragas and raginis:
But what have they ever received
from Hari?

Death enshrouds
the whole world,
including all
the superstitious wisemen.
Kabir, say,
"Only those will be freed
who find
the path of love."

4

I watch with both my eyes
and I see nothing but Hari.
My eyes are filled with love:
I can speak nothing.

Doubts and fear have vanished:
I have placed Ram's name in my heart. (Rest)

The Actor sounds the drum;
the people come out
to see the show.
Then the Actor ends the play —
that is His enjoyment.

Words cannot rid doubt;
the world is tired of mere talk.
He blends in the hearts

of those to whom He reveals Himself,
through your guru's teaching.

If your guru is merciful, heart and soul
will blend with Hari.
Kabir, say,
"Those who meet Jagjivan, the Giver,
are dyed in love's color."

5

If holy books are streams of milk,
then the company of sages
is the churn.
If you churn in that company,
no one will deny you the whey.

Girl, why don't you marry Ram:
He is Jagjivan, the soul's staff. (Rest)

Your neck is in an iron ring,
fetters are on your feet:
Ram makes you wander from house to house —
yet still you don't understand.
Poor girl, Yama has his eye on you.

Prabhu is the root and cause
of all things;
what's really in your own hands, poor girl?
You have to get up, though half-asleep,
and do what you're told.

Girl, who gave you this advice
with which you erased
illusion's trace?
This is how Kabir found real bliss:
My heart exults in the Guru's grace.

6

Find Him
without whom you cannot live,
and fulfill all your desires.
Everlasting life is best, they say:
Without death
there can be no life.

What more wisdom can there be:
As we look, things change. (Rest)

You grind saffron and sandalwood,
mixing them together.
Without eyes, you see the world:
A son begets his father,
a city is built
where there was no room.

The beggar has found the Provider,
and he can't eat all
that he is given;
he doesn't want to leave the food,
nor can he finish it —
why should he now go elsewhere?

Those who know
how to die for life
will delight in holy peace,
boundless as a mountain.
I, Kabir, have found the treasure:
Upon meeting Hari, I vanished.

7

Why read?
Why meditate?
Why listen to the Vedas or the Puranas?

What use is reading and listening,
if you don't naturally
yearn for Him?

Fool, you never repeat Hari's name;
what are you racking your brains for? (Rest)

In darkness
you need a lamp,
if you want to find the Unreachable.
When you find the Unreachable,
the lamp will burn
in your heart forever.

Kabir, say, "Now I understand—
and my heart soars.
But people are not content
with just a happy heart;
and if they are not,
what can you do?"

8

Malice in your heart—
wisdom on your lips.
Liar, why are you churning water?

Why scrub your body
when the filth is within? (Rest)

If you were to wash a gourd
in all the holy places,
it would still be bitter.

After meditating,
say this, Kabir, "O Murari,
bear me across this world's ocean."

9

With cunning you gather wealth
belonging to others,

and then you squander it
on your wife and son.

O my heart, do not deceive others,
even by mistake:
You'll have to pay with your life
at the final reckoning. (Rest)

Your body weakens every minute,
and old age peers out —
no one is going to pour
even water on your hands then.

Kabir says,
"You cannot call anyone your own;
repeat Ram's name in your heart
all the time."

10

O sages, my mind,
restless as the wind,
is now bound by solace.
It is now ready to accept
whatever there may be. (Rest)

My guru has shown me
how stealthily
wild animals wandered in.
I have shut the gates —
and lutes play unplucked.

The lotus-pitcher was filled with water;
when I straightened it,
the water spilled out.
O slave Kabir, say, "I understand;
and now my heart is happy."

11

It's hard to be a devotee
when you're hungry.

Here, take back Your rosary.
I ask only for the dust
from the feet of sages,
so I may be a burden to no one.

O Madho, how can I live
if I am ashamed of You.
If You do not give,
then I shall have to beg. (Rest)

I ask only
for four pounds of flour,
half a pound of butter,
and some salt.
I ask only for a pound of lentils,
which can feed me twice a day.

I ask only
for a four-legged cot,
a pillow, a mattress,
and a quilt to keep me covered.
And then Your slave
will serve with love.

I have never coveted;
I am fond of Your name only.
Kabir, say,
"My heart is happy;
and when my heart is happy,
I understand Hari."

From Raga Dhanashri

1

Sanaka, Sanandana, Mahesha,
Sheshnaga, and others
never learned Your secret.

I have placed Ram in my heart
by being in the company of sages. (Rest)

Hanuman and Garuda,
Surpati and mighty kings
never realized Your virtues.

The four Vedas, the Smriti, the Puranas,
Kamla's lord and Kamla
never really understood.

Kabir, say, "They who touch Ram's feet
and stay under His protection
will never wander."

2

From days to hours, hours to minutes,
life lessens, the body weakens.
Death the stalker prowls like a hunter—
tell me, what can you do?

That day draws near.
Mother, father, brother, son, wife:
Tell me, to whom do you belong? (Rest)

An animal does not know its own self,
while it has breath in its body:
It is greedy for more and more life—
its eyes see nothing.

Kabir, say, "Listen, O mortal,
put aside all doubts in your heart.
Repeat only His name,
and enter His shelter, O mortal."

3

Those who know a little about love—
you call them strange.
As water once blended with water
cannot again be separated,
so the weaver, by being humble,
was absorbed.

O Hari's people,
I have a simple mind.
If you die in Benares,
what does Ram owe you, O Kabir? (Rest)

Kabir says,
"Listen, O people,
what is Benares,
what is barren Magahar,
if Ram
is in your hearts?"

4

Shallow devotion will get you
to Indra's city or Shiva's city—
but you would have to
come right back out again.

What should I ask for? Nothing lasts forever:
Place Ram's name in your heart. (Rest)

Son, wife,
great wealth:
Tell me,
who ever was comforted by these?

Kabir says,
"Nothing is of use to me:
Ram's name is wealth enough
for my soul."

5

Remember Ram, remember Ram,
remember Ram, O my brother.
So many have drowned
without remembering Ram's name. (Rest)

Wife, son, body, house, wealth
are pleasureable —
but not really yours to keep:
Death comes in the end all the same.

Ajamala, the elephant,
and the prostitute sinned;
still they crossed over
by repeating Ram's name.

You lurked in the wombs
of pigs and dogs — and still
you are not ashamed. You abandoned
Ram's name: You should have poisoned yourself.

Abandon things you should do
and the things you should not do,
and take the name of Ram.
By the guru's grace, O slave Kabir, love Ram.

From Raga Tilang

1

The Vedas and the Western holy books
are exaggerations, O my brother:
they do not ease the heart.
If you stop and think
for just one minute,
you will know that Khuda is everywhere.

O man, search your heart every day.
Why do you go around perplexed?
You cannot grasp this magic-show world
in your hands. (Rest)

You are happy reading lies,
and then like fools
you quibble over them.
The only true Master
lives inside the people,
not in the idol of Krishna.

The river flows
in the sky;
you should have bathed in it.
Become his fakir;
rub your eyes
and see — He is everywhere.

Allah is the holiest of holies;
If there were someone else,
I would be skeptical.
Kabir, Karim's mercy is only understood
by those to whom He grants
understanding.

167

From Raga Suhi

1

What have you really done
after being born?
You never once
took Ram's name.

You don't worship Ram.
What are you really doing?
How are you preparing for death,
O miserable fool? (Rest)

In hardship and happiness
you raised your family;
when you die,
you alone will suffer.

When you're grabbed by the neck,
you will scream.
Kabir, say, "Why didn't you think
in the first place?"

2

She shudders and trembles like a child:
"I don't know how my husband will treat me."

Night has gone; don't let day go by too.
Bumblebees leave; cranes now alight and sit. (Rest)

An unfired pitcher will not hold water:
The swan has left; the body wilts.

A young virgin adorns herself—
but she can never know bliss without a lover.

My arms are tired of scaring off crows;
Kabir, say, "This tale is almost over."

3

Your time for deeds is over;
now you must give account.
Yama's cruel messengers
have come to take you away:
"What did you earn?
How did you squander it?
Come quickly,
the Master calls.

"Come at once, the Master calls.
The summons from Hari's court has come." (Rest)

You will grovel:
"But I have things still to do
in the village. Let me settle them
by this evening. I will pay
for all your expenses;
and we can say
our dawn prayers
on the road."

Those who are infused
with Hari's color
by associating with sages
are twice blessed and most fortunate.
They will be happy in this world
and the next—
for they have won
that priceless object of all birth.

Those who sleep while awake
are not reborn.
The wealth and fortune
you amassed
is not really yours.
Kabir, say, "Those who forget
the Master lie neglected
in the dust."

From Raga Suhi-Lalit

4

Eyes are tired;
tired are ears of listening;
tired is this beautiful body.
Just a slight nod of old age,
and all your senses grow tired —
Maya alone never tires.

Fool, you never learned to discern;
uselessly you squandered your life. (Rest)

O mortal, remember Him
as long as there is breath
in your body.
Though you lose your body,
lose not your love:
Live close to Hari's feet.

Those in whom He plants the Word,
lose their thirst.
Make understanding of His command
your dice,
and conquest of the heart,
your throw.

Nothing of theirs will be destroyed
who realize and worship
the invisible One.
Kabir, say,
"Those who know how to throw
the dice, never lose."

5

One fort, five lords:
All five demand revenues.
I did not sow their land:
Difficult is this tax to render.

O people of Hari, the accountant
threatens me continually.
Throwing up my hands,
I called on my guru, and he saved me. (Rest)

Nine surveyors, and ten quick judges;
they don't leave the tenants in peace.
They never measure with a full tape;
they take countless bribes.

The One who lives in seventy-two houses,
His name my guru wrote as the tax.
And when I checked in at Dharmraja's office,
I found I didn't owe a penny.

Never slander saints—
for the saints and Ram are one.
Kabir, say, "I have found that Guru
whose very name is divine knowledge."

From Raga Bilawal

1

Such is the world
that none can stay on,
O my brother.
Walk on the straight path;
otherwise you will be shoved aside,
O my brother. (Rest)

Children, the young and old,
O my brother,
all will be driven off by Yama.
A poor man is a mouse:
The tomcat Death gobbles him up,
O my brother.

He doesn't care
if a man's rich or poor,
O my brother:
He slaughters both the ruler and the ruled —
so strong is Death,
O my brother.

Hari's servants — those whom He likes —
theirs is a different story,
O my brother:
They neither come nor go,
nor die — Parbrahma is their friend,
O my brother.

Wife, son, prestige, wealth —
forsake them all,
O my life.

175

Kabir says, "Listen, O you sages,
there's no other way to meet Sarangpani,
O my brothers."

2

I do not read learned books,
nor do I know how to debate.
I have gone mad
hearing and speaking
the virtues of Hari.

O Father, I am mad.
The whole world is wise,
but I am mad.
I have wasted myself away;
do not let others do the same. (Rest)

I did not
drive myself mad—
Ram drove me mad.
The True Guru
has burned away my doubts.

When I became mad
I lost
all my senses;
others need not
copy my mistakes.

Those who don't know themselves
are mad.
When you recognize yourself,
you recognize
the One.

If you're not drunk yet,
you'll never
be drunk.
Kabir, say,
"I am infused with Ram's color."

3

Leaving your home,
you go to the forest,
gathering and eating roots.
Still your sinful, evil heart
does not forsake impiety.

How can I be saved?
How can I get across?
Terrible and vast is this world-ocean.
Save me, save me, O Beethal,
Your slave is in Your hands. (Rest)

There are so many pleasures—
hard it is to give them up.
I try so much
to stay away from them;
yet again and again they enfold me.

Gone is youth,
gone, even old age:
Not once have I done good.
By associating with cowries,
my priceless life became like them.

Kabir, say,
"O my Madho,
You are all-pervasive.
None equals Your mercy—
none equals my sin."

4

This weaver is forever
fetching his clay-pot,
forever plastering his kitchen.
He cares not for his loom or shuttle;
he is raptured by the bliss
of saying "Hari, Hari."

In our family, whoever said "Ram?"
Ever since this son of mine
has gotten hold of a rosary,
we've had no peace. (Rest)

O my oldest and youngest
sisters-in-law,
listen—
it's really an amazing thing—
this boy has lost all the hanks of yarn.
I wish he would die.

The Swami of all bliss
is the one Hari;
my guru has given me His name.
He preserved the honor of saint Prahlada,
and ripped apart Harnakhasa
with His claws.

I have abandoned the household gods
and the traditions of my fathers.
I have been given the Word by my guru.
Kabir says,
"He smashes all sin;
He saves His saints."

5

No raja equals Hari.
Rajas live and display their grandeur
for a few days only. (Rest)

If we are Your slaves,
we need not falter:
You engulf the three worlds.
No one can lay hands on us:
None dares even to speak
in front of us.

Think and think again,
O my heart,

and music, unstruck, will play.
Kabir, say, "My doubts and fears
have vanished. He protected
Dhruva and Prahlada."

6

Save me,
for I have done evil:
I have not been gentle,
I have not done my duty,
I have not worshipped nor served,
I have been proud,
I have walked the crooked path. (Rest)

I have cherished this body,
believing it to be immortal—
this fragile, unfired clay-pot.
I forgot Him—
who, through His mercy,
gave me life—
and fell in with others.

I am a thief to You;
don't call me a saint.
I fall at Your feet for shelter.
Kabir, say, "Listen to this:
Send not the message of Yama
to me."

7

I am a supplicant at Your court:
None but You look after me.
Fling open the door
and show Yourself to me. (Rest)

You are the Master of wealth,
the unstinting Giver.
With my own ears
I hear Your praise.

From whom should I beg?
All those whom I see
have nothing to give.
You alone can get me across.

Jaidev and Namdev,
and the Brahmin Sudama—
You showed mercy to them
without end.
Kabir, say, "You have the might
to bestow all things;
You can grant all the four blessings
without delay."

8

A staff, earrings, patched cloak,
and a begging pouch—
you're wandering in superstition,
dressed up as a yogi.

Forget your yogic posture, fool,
and breath-suspensions.
Leave this chicanery, fool,
and worship Hari. (Rest)

The things you beg for
are the leavings of the three worlds.
Kabir, say, "Only Keshava
is the real Yogi."

9

O Jagdish, O Gosain,
Maya has made us wander away
from Your feet.
Not one measure of love
flickers within us.
What can we poor people do? (Rest)

Cursed is this body, cursed is wealth,
and cursed, Maya.
Doubly cursed are reason and intellect,
which deceive people.
Keep Maya well in check;
keep her tied up, according to Your word.

What use is farming or trading?
False is worldly pride.
Kabir, say,
"Many will be sorry in the end
when death
finally comes."

10

In the pool of the body
a matchless lotus grows:
The supreme light of Purushotama,
without form, without shape.

O my heart, praise Hari.
Abandon doubts: Ram is the world's soul. (Rest)

No one has seen it
flower or wilt.
It dies where it is born,
like the leaves of a water-lily.

When I thought of eternal peace,
I forsook Maya, seeing that she was fatal.
Kabir, say, "Serve Him—
the Murari that is in your heart."

11

Love for Gobind scattered my doubts
about birth and death.
I have blended into eternal Silence,
though I am still alive. (Rest)

The sound
born of bronze
again blends with bronze.
When the bronze cracks,
hey, pundit,
where does the sound go?

I have seen Him
where the three breaths meet:
Each pore has awakened.
Such insight have I gained
that I have forsaken all things,
though I am still alive.

I have come to know
my own reality.
My light has blended with Light.
Kabir, say,
"I understand finally:
My heart has blended with Gobind."

12

Why should they waver,
O Deva,
in whose hearts
rest Your lotus-like feet.
All solace,
all treasures are theirs
who slowly, ceaselessly say,
"O Deva." (Rest)

You shall acquire insight
to see Him in all things,
when that hard knot
is unloosened by Deva.
You shall hinder Maya
again and again
when you weigh your heart
in the scales of Deva.

Wherever you go,
you shall find solace—
and Maya will never trip you up.
Kabir, say,
"My heart is happy,
ever since it was absorbed
into love
for Ram."

From Raga Gaund

1

When you meet a sage,
ask something and listen.
When you meet a non-believer
keep perfectly silent.

Father, if I speak,
what shall I say?
Something like:
"Stay close to Ram's name." (Rest)

Speaking to sages
leads to something good.
Talking to fools
is just useless shouting.

Endless chatter
increases evil;
yet how can you think,
if you don't speak?

Kabir, say, "An empty vessel
makes much noise;
a full one
never makes a sound."

2

When a man dies,
he is of no use.
When an animal dies,
it's put to many uses.

185

How can I know the outcome of my deeds?
How can I know, O Father? (Rest)

Bones burn
like a bundle of sticks;
hair burns
like a handful of grass.

Kabir, say,
"Only then does a man wake up
when Yama's club
smashes his pate."

3

In the realm of the sky,
in the realm of the underworld,
in all the four realms that we see,
He is present.
Purushotama is ever
the root of all joy.
The body may perish,
but the realm lasts forever.

I have given up everything;
and now I am wondering
where life comes from.
Where does it vanish? (Rest)

The five elements blended
to form the body:
Who mixed them together,
O my brother?
You say life is bound to one's actions:
Who gave life
to these actions,
O my brother?

The body is in Hari,
Hari is in the body—

He is blended inseparably
in each thing, O my brother.
Kabir, say, "I will not let go
of Ram's name.
Everything that happens
is spontaneous, O my brother."

4

They tied my hands
and tossed me
like a clump of dirt.
In their anger,
they hit the elephant
on the head.
The elephant screamed
and ran away.
I could sacrifice myself
for that animal.

O my Thakur, You are my strength.
The qazi said, "Goad that elephant on, (Rest)

hey, mahout,
or else
I'll have your head
cut off!
Make it move!
Hit it! Hit it!"
The elephant did not move.
It was enraptured:
In its heart
lived the Dispenser of Treasure.

"What sin
has this saint committed
that you tie him up
like a bundle
and toss him in front of the elephant?"
The elephant again and again

picked up this bundle
and bowed in obeisance to it.
Still the blind qazi
could not figure it out.

He tried
three times—
but still
his cruel heart
was not satisfied.
Kabir, say,
"Gobind is mine.
His slave's life
has reached
the fourth stage."

5

He is neither man nor god;
neither a pure ascetic
nor a worshipper of Shiva;
neither a yogi nor a hermit.
He has no mother;
he is no one's son.

Who dwells here in this house,
whom no one can fathom? (Rest)

He is neither a householder,
nor a mendicant-saint;
he is neither a king nor a beggar;
he has neither body,
nor a drop of blood;
he is neither a Brahmin nor a Kshatriya.

He is neither an austere sage,
nor a sheikh;
he is neither born nor dies.
They who mourn
at his death,
shall lose their honor.

By the guru's grace,
I have found the right path.
My birth and death have been erased.
Kabir, say,
"It's hard to erase the light of Ram,
like ink from paper."

6

The thread breaks;
the starch is used up—
the door hangs
from its hinges.
All the glue brushes are falling apart:
Death looms
over this bald-headed sage.

This bald-headed sage
can't hold on to money.
I've had it up to here
with all these ascetics
coming in and going out. (Rest)

The loom and the shuttle
lie forgotten:
His heart is full of Ram's name
day and night.
There's nothing to eat
for his own son and daughter—
only the bald-heads leave here full.

Some are inside the house,
some are on their way;
we get the floor,
they get the bed.
They stroke their pates
and carry books in their pouches;
we get roasted chickpeas,
they get the fine bread.

All these bald-heads
have become one;
these bald-heads
are the support of the drowning.
Listen, O blind,
guruless Loi,
Kabir has accepted the protection
of these bald-heads.

7

The husband dies,
but the wife does not weep:
Another man looks after her.
When he in turn dies,
hell looms before him
for pleasures enjoyed here.

One bride is loved by all the world;
she is the wife of all living things. (Rest)

Wearing a necklace,
the bride looks alluring:
Poison to the sage, pleasing to the world.
Wearing make-up she sits like a whore;
she wanders all wretched
cursed by the saints.

When sages flee from her,
she chases after;
by the guru's grace
she is afraid of being beaten.
She is the life and soul of the godless;
to me she looks like an ogre.

When the godly guru came
and met me in his kindness,
I found out her many secrets.
Kabir, say,
"I have turned her out;
the world is stuck with her now."

8

O my brother,
if there is no wealth
in the house, guests
must go away hungry.
The householder
is not happy;
he is blamed for everything,
being without a bride.

Hail the bride,
for she is most holy;
she has changed the minds
of many sages. (Rest)

This bride
is a miser's daughter;
forsaking His servants,
she sleeps with all the world.
There she stands
at the sage's door:
"I seek your protection —
save me."

This bride
is extremely beautiful;
her anklets jingle, jingle
as she walks.
As long as man has breath
she will embrace him;
if he refuses,
she must flee barefoot.

The three worlds
are in this bride's grip;
she loves the eighteen Puranas
and places of pilgrimage.
She has ensnared
Brahma, Vishnu, Maheshwara;
she has pierced the hearts
of kings and maharajas.

This bride
has no limits:
She is in league
with the five Naradas.
When the clay-pots
of these Naradas are shattered,
Kabir, say,
"I was released by my guru's grace."

9

As a house cannot stand
without beams,
so how can you cross over
without His name?
You cannot hold water
without a jar,
so without a sage,
you cannot be saved.

Burn those who do not think about Ram,
whose mind and body are sunk in worldly joys. (Rest)

As without a ploughman,
earth cannot be seeded,
so how can you string jewels
without thread?
How can you tie a knot
without making a loop—
so without a sage,
you cannot be saved.

As a child cannot be born
without a father and mother,
so how can you wash clothes
without water?
How do you ride
without a horse—
so without a sage
you cannot be saved.

As without music
there cannot be dancing,
so a widow is forever parted
from her husband.
Kabir, say,
"There is only one thing worth doing:
Become the Guru's slave
and never die again."

10

He too is a pimp
who beats his heart,
and in so doing,
escapes from Yama.
He hammers his heart,
then tests it with a touchstone —
such a pimp
will secure salvation.

Hey, world, whom are you calling a pimp?
Words can have many meanings. (Rest)

She too is a whore
who dances with her soul,
who is not diverted by falsehood,
who is gratified with truth,
and who completes
the rhythm of her soul.
God is the keeper of this whore's soul.

She too is a streetwalker
who looks after her own bazaar,
who lights
her five torches,
who welcomes
the service of Naunayak.
I acknowledge that streetwalker
as my guru.

He too is a thief
who is not malevolent,
who speaks His name
in order to control his senses.
By his mercy
I have obtained virtue:
Blessed is this holy guru;
he is handsome, he is clever.

11

Blessed is Gopal,
blessed the holy guru;
blessed is grain
which makes the hearts
of the hungry blossom.
Blessed are the sages
who understand all this:
They will go to meet Sarangpani.

Grain comes from the Primal Being;
repeat His name when you taste grain. (Rest)

Worship His name,
worship grain:
How beautiful is its color
when it blends with water.
Those who stay away from grain
shall lose their esteem
in the three worlds.

She who forsakes grain
and engages in deceit
is neither a bride
nor a whore.
Those who jabber
that they live only on milk
secretly eat
entire loaves at once.

No one can be happy
without grain;
you cannot meet Gopal
by giving up eating grain.
Kabir, say,
"This is what I know:
Blessed is grain by which the heart
is satisfied with Thakur."

From Raga Ramkali

1

My body is a cask
in which I mix the yeast;
I have made my guru's word
raw sugar, O my brothers.
I have peeled and cut up
desire, lust, anger, pride, malice,
and mixed them with the sugar,
O my brothers.

Show me a sage lost in peace,
O my brothers, and I will pay him
homage and penance as commission.
I will give body and soul
for a drop from his still,
O my brothers. (Rest)

I have made the fourteen worlds
my furnace, in which I have lit
the fire of Brahma,
O my brothers.
I have made sweet song
the plug for the worm,
and my heart's song the condensation,
O my brothers.

Pilgrimage, fasting, precepts, purifications,
asceticism, the breath of my two nostrils —
these I have placed as my capital,
O my brothers.
I have made understanding my cup

197

for that rare liquor:
It is this great ambrosia that I drink,
O my brothers.

A most pure trickle
streams down,
and my soul becomes steeped
in that ambrosia.
Kabir, say, "All other drinks
have no punch—
this great juice is perfect,
O my brothers."

2

Make knowledge your raw sugar,
meditation your *mahua* flowers,
and fear of God your furnace.
Then if you drink
you will know the bliss
known by those who suspend breath.

Hey, yogi, my soul is drunk;
I am drunk.
I have tasted that heady juice:
The three worlds are become luminous. (Rest)

Joining the two millstones,
I lit the furnace.
Now I drink the best extract.
I burn lust and anger,
and love for the world
slips away.

Wisdom's radiance was revealed to me
by my guru, acquainted with God.
I received understanding from the True Guru.
The slave Kabir
is drunk with His liquor—
this drunkenness will never wear off.

3

O Swami,
You are my Mount Meru.
I have sought Your refuge.
You shall never quake,
and I shall not fall—
Hari is my keeper.

Then as now, and ever always: You, You.
By Your grace, I am forever blissful. (Rest)

Leaning on you I came
and started to live in Magahar:
You cooled my burning body.
I first saw You in Magahar;
only then did I go to Benares.

Magahar is the same as Benares;
for me they're both
the same.
A poor man like me
has found the treasure:
The proud die in their pride.

The proud are pricked by thorns—
and they have no one
to take out those thorns.
All their lives they cry out in pain
as though they were burning
in black hell.

What is hell
and wretched heaven:
Both are deemed worthless
by the sages.
I do not need anyone's help—
by my guru's grace.

I have ascended
the throne

and met Sarangpani.
Ram and Kabir
have become one —
no one can tell them apart.

4

I rout evil by respecting sages —
that is my ordinance.
Day and night I am at Your feet,
fanning You
with the fan of my heart.

I am a dog at Your court:
I stick out my snout and howl away. (Rest)

In all my former lives
I have been Your servant:
I cannot stop being one now.
Sweet love was branded on my forehead
at Your door.

Those branded die as martyrs
in the field;
the unbranded run away.
Saints are those who know how to serve —
and Hari puts them all in His treasury.

In the fine little house
is the most beautiful room for meditation.
The guru has given Kabir a precious object:
"Take this
and keep it safe."

Kabir gave it to the world —
take it, who can.
She who drinks
the divine ambrosia
will have an everlasting marriage.

5

Why have you forgotten Him, O Brahmin,
whose mouth first spoke
the Vedas and the Gayatri.
Why do you, O pundit, not call Him Hari,
whose feet touch the whole world.

Why, O Brahmin, do you not say, "Hari?"
You never say, "Ram"—
so you suffer hell's pains. (Rest)

You call yourself high-caste,
but you eat at the expense
of the low-caste:
You fill your belly
by doing wayward deeds.

On the fourteenth and fifteenth
of each month,
you make up stories in order to beg—
although you carry a lamp,
you still fall into the well.

You are a Brahmin,
I, a weaver from Benares.
How can we be equal?
I rose by saying Ram's name;
you sank, O pundit, clutching the Vedas.

6

One tree,
yet countless shoots and branches;
its leaves are filled with nectar.
This is the garden of ambrosia,
O my brother—
the perfect Hari planted it.

Only those few,
those very few holy ones,
know the tale of Raja Ram,
O my brother,
in whose heart
His light gleams. (Rest)

A bumblebee
drunk with nectar
loses himself in the full-blown petals;
but fanning the air
he flits away
to the sky.

From the gentle silence
a beautiful plant sprouts,
which soaks up
the waters of the earth.
Kabir, say, "I serve those
who have seen this plant."

7

Make peace your earrings,
mercy your begging bag,
meditation your begging bowl.
I have sewn my beggar's blanket
for my body;
my staff is His name, O yogi.

O yogi,
practise that yoga
which lets you worship
and do penance,
while you enjoy yourself,
through the guru's guidance. (Rest)

Make wisdom the ash
to smear on your body,
and blending of your consciousness with God's

your little trumpet-horn.
Forsaking all, wander in your body's city,
playing the rebeck of your heart.

Take and place
the five virtues
in your heart—
such meditation lasts forever.
Kabir says, "Listen, O you sages,
make righteousness and mercy your gardens."

8

For what purpose were we born in the world?
What good was our birth?
Never once did we think of Him
who slakes all our desires
and bears us across the world's ocean.

O Gobind, so heartless are we
that we never loved or adored Prabhu
who gave us body and soul. (Rest)

We never gave up lusting
after other men's wealth and women;
we gossiped and quarrelled.
We died and were born again and again—
this tussle never ends.

Not even for a minute
did we go to that house
where Hari's saints gathered to speak.
We spent all our time with whores,
thieves, panders, drunkards.

Our greatest treasures were
lust, anger, pride, greed.
We never even dreamed
of mercy, righteousness,
and the Guru's service.

O Dindayal, Kirpal, Damodar,
Beloved of Your servants,
O Router of fear,
Kabir says, "Protect Your poor slave.
I shall serve You, O Hari."

9

Meditation leads to salvation's door:
Go to heaven—
why go back to the world?
In the house of the fearless One,
where music, unstruck, sounds,
you shall play trumpets.

Meditate upon Him in your heart.
Without meditation there is no salvation. (Rest)

Unfettered meditation
brings salvation:
Your heavy load is taken off.
Welcome Him in your heart,
so you will not be born
again and again.

Blissful meditation
will light a lamp inside you
that does not need any oil.
This lamp will make you immortal;
this lamp will draw out the poison
of lust and anger.

Pierce this meditation
that gives you salvation,
and wear it around your neck.
Never take it off.
Meditate always:
Your guru's grace will get you across.

Meditation will free you
from dependence on others:

You will sleep on silken sheets at home.
Your heart will be at peace;
your life will blossom:
Deeply drink this meditation.

This meditation
will erase your blemishes;
you will be free from Maya's touch.
Meditate, meditate, and sing,
"Hari, Hari." You will obtain
this meditation from your true guru.

Always, always meditate day and night:
When you rise, when you lie down,
when you breathe in, when you breathe out.
Waking or sleeping,
relish the taste of meditation—
meditation will bring union.

Meditation will remove
all your burdens;
meditation upon Ram's name
will become your support.
Kabir, say, "He is limitless.
Chants and mantras are useless before Him."

10

The binder is bound;
the savior Guru has put out the fire.
Carefully I looked at myself—
from the soles of my feet
to the top of my head—
and I was cleansed.

To be blended with Pavanpati
is the highest state:
No death, no birth, no old age. (Rest)

I no longer rely on Maya;
my dwelling place

is now in the sky.
I have entered the snake's circle:
Without doubt
I have met the Raja.

Gone are my worldly longings:
The moon has swallowed the sun.
When I joined together
all my breaths completely,
I heard the lyre play,
without being plucked.

The teacher spoke the Word.
Immediately I placed it
in my heart.
By saying, "Creator, Creator,"
you will cross over:
Kabir has given away the secret.

11

The moon and the sun
are both bodies of light.
In the light
is the unparalleled Brahma.

O wisemen, ponder upon Brahma:
All creation is contained in that Light. (Rest)

Behold the diamond:
I bow before it.
Kabir says,
"Niranjan is indescribable."

12

Hey, world,
be vigilant, be alert.
You're being robbed,
though you're wide awake,
O my brothers.

While the Vedas
and the Shastras
look on —
watchful guards both —
Yama leads you away. (Rest)

The margosa
becomes a mango tree,
the mango
a margosa tree,
and the banana tree
becomes a thorn bush.
The fruit of the coconut
becomes a ripe pod
of the silk tree.
Think, O fools and simpletons.

Hari is sugar
scattered upon sand:
Elephants
can't gather it up.
Kabir, say,
"Renounce family,
caste, ancestors —
become an ant,
gather up that sugar —
and eat."

From Raga Maru

1

Hey, pundit,
whose bad advice
are you following?
You and your family
are all going to drown
because you never worshipped Ram,
O luckless fool. (Rest)

What use is reading
the Vedas and the Puranas?
You only become burdened
like a donkey.
You never learned the reality
of Ram's name—
how will you get across?

You take life
and call it being religious.
Tell me, my brother,
what then is being irreligious?
You call yourself a saint—
whom do you call
a butcher?

O blind-hearted one,
you don't even know your own self—
how can you teach others,
O my brother?
You sell knowledge
just to make money—
you're wasting your life.

Narada has said the same thing;
Vyasa's words are similar—
go and even ask Sukhdeva:
Kabir, say, "You will be released
if you meditate upon Ram.
If you don't, you'll drown,
O my brother."

2

How can you meet Him
by living in forests?
You have yet to remove
the evil from your heart.
Those who see
their own homes as forests
will achieve perfection
in this world.

Only Ram can bestow real peace:
Lovingly adore Ram in your heart. (Rest)

Why mat your long hair
with ash?
Why go and live
in caves?
If you conquer your heart,
you have conquered the world:
In this way
you will be freed from Maya.

Many people
put antimony
on their eyes—
but for different reasons.
The eyes
that wear the antimony
of divine wisdom
see truth.

Kabir, say,
"Now I know;
my guru's wisdom
has allowed me
to understand.
I have found Hari
inside my own heart—
I need roam no longer."

3

You say
you have acquired
wealth and spiritual power.
So why do you
still depend upon others?
How you can make such claims—
I'm ashamed to say.

Those who have found Ram,
do not beg from door to door. (Rest)

This false world
prowls around
in the hope of using wealth
for a few days.
Those who have drunk
the water of Ram
will never again
be thirsty.

Those who have discovered
the path,
by their guru's grace,
move beyond hope
and hopelessness.
Those who turn away
from worldly things
see truth everywhere.

Those who have tasted
the nectar of Ram's name
are borne across
by Hari's name.
Kabir, say,
"They become purified gold.
Their wandering is banished
to this ocean's farthest shore."

4

As rain and the sea
become one upon merging;
as ripples and the stream
become one upon blending—
so my silence
becomes absorbed into the Infinite—
none can tell us apart—
I am become air.

Why should I return? It is His decree
that we come and go. But I have found Him
who gave this decree—
and have merged with Him. (Rest)

When this creation
of five elements
reaches its end,
then also all my doubts
shall end.
I have given up differentiating:
I see everyone the same.
I meditate upon His name.

I can only do
what I came here to do—
thus I earn
good deeds.
If Hari is merciful,

then I shall unite
with Him,
by my guru's grace.

If you are dead,
though you live—
you shall live when you die:
Never again will you be reborn.
Kabir, say,
"Those who are steeped in His name—
their love will blend
with the infinite Silence."

5

If you tell me
to go away,
then first show me the path
to salvation.
The One in many:
You are in all things.
Why do you make me doubt?

O Ram, you carry me over—
but where are you taking me?
I ask, when will you save me?
What kind of salvation
are you giving me?
Have I not already obtained it,
by Your grace? (Rest)

We say, "Going across;
being carried over,"
as long as we don't know
the real truth.
But my heart
has become pure.
Kabir, say, "My soul exults."

6

Fortresses and castles
made of gold —
all these Ravana
left behind.

Why do you act as you please?
When Yama comes and grabs you
by the hair, only Hari's name
will then get you freed. (Rest)

The Master ordained
deathless Death,
and the binding snares
of this deceitful world.

Kabir, say,
"In the end only those
who have Ram, the core of all things,
in their hearts will be saved."

7

The body is a village,
the soul its landowner.
In it live five farmers:
Eyes, nose, ears, tongue, genitals —
they never listen to what they're told.

O my Father,
I cannot live
in this village anymore:
Chitragupta, the accountant,
wants each moment accounted for. (Rest)

When Dharmrai asks for my account,
I'll have to pay dearly.
The five farmers have run away,
and the royal land stewards
have handcuffed the soul.

Kabir says, "Listen, O you sages,
let's settle things in the field.
Forgive Your slave just this once,
so I won't have to return
to this horrid ocean of the world."

8

None has seen Him,
O *vairagi;*
when you are free from fear,
that's when
you can see Him,
yes, oh yes.

When you realize He exists
in all things, then you'll fear Him,
O *vairagi.*
When you perceive His command,
you'll be free from fear,
yes, oh yes.

Do not use Hari
for outward show,
O *vairagi:*
The whole world
is busy doing that,
yes, oh yes.

Thirst never
leaves you,
O *vairagi,*
and anxiety
burns your body,
yes, oh yes.

When you burn worries,
you burn
the body,

O *vairagi*—
so kill your heart,
yes, oh yes.

You can't be a *vairagi*
without the True Guru,
O *vairagi*—
though everyone
wants to be one,
yes, oh yes.

If He is kind,
you'll meet the True Guru,
O *vairagi*,
and you'll acquire
that state of bliss,
yes, oh yes.

Kabir, say,
"Pray for one thing only,
O *vairagi*:
Take me across
this horrid ocean of the world,
yes, oh yes."

9

O king, who wants to come to you?
I received so much love from Vidura
that my heart is pleased
with this poor man. (Rest)

Beholding all your elephants,
you've forgotten yourself:
You did not recognize
the Lord Krishna.
You have milk—
but the water at Vidura's place
seemed like ambrosia to me.

His boiled vegetables
equalled the daintiest of your puddings.
We passed the night
singing hymns of praise.
Kabir's Master is blissful
and full of joy:
He doesn't care for anyone's caste.

Slokas from Raga Maru

I

The kettle drum echoes in the sky:
Aim is taken, wounds given.
The warrior stands fast on the field—
now is the time to fight.

II

Recognize Him as a true warrior
who fights for the poor.
Even though he is hacked to death,
he never flees the field.

10

You have forgotten your religion,
O fool, you have forgotten your religion:
You gorge your belly
and sleep like an animal—
you've wasted your human birth. (Rest)

You never spoke
with sages;
you practised deceit:
You will roam like
dogs, pigs, and crows.

Because of your works, words, thoughts,
you see yourself as high and mighty

and others as beneath you.
People like you
I've seen going to hell.

The wrathful,
lechers, deceivers,
thugs, and idlers
all speak evil about others—
never do they remember Ram.

Kabir, say,
"Fools, simpletons,
and the vulgar
do not know the name of Ram—
how will they get across?"

11

Remember Ram, O my soul,
or you will regret it.
O my sinful heart,
you are greedy—
don't you know
you'll have to leave
today or tomorrow? (Rest)

You're wasting your birth
by being greedy:
Maya is fooling you.
Don't pride yourself
on your youth and wealth:
They will crumble
like old paper.

When Yama comes,
grabs you by the hair,
and thrashes you on the floor,
nothing is going to work then.
You were never merciful,
you never meditated or worshipped:
You're going to get your face smashed.

When Dharmrai
asks you for an account,
what will you show him?
Kabir says,
"Listen, O you sages,
you can swim across
with the band of saints."

From Raga Kedara

1

Flattery and fault-finding
are both evil:
Abandon pride and arrogance.
Those who see no difference
between iron and gold
are the very image of Bhagwan.

Few are Your servants.
Abandon lust, anger,
and worldly love —
only then
can you behold
the feet of Hari. (Rest)

What we call
the true virtues
are all part of Your Maya.
Those who perceive
the fourth virtue
obtain the highest state.

They no longer feel the need
to go on pilgrimages,
to fast, to purify themselves,
to practice austerities.
When they think about Ram
desire, Maya, and doubts vanish.

Darkness flees
from the house
where a lamp is lit,

and doubts vanish.
Then only can you live without fear;
thus speaks Kabir, the servant, the slave.

2

Some sell copper and bronze,
some cloves and betel nuts;
sages sell Gobind's name:
And such are my wares.

O traders in Hari's name
you hold the precious diamond
in your hands—
let go of all things worldly. (Rest)

Those given truth hold on to it—
they are traders in truth.
They load up their wares
and take them to the Storekeeper.

He is the ruby, the jewel, the gem,
and He Himself the dealer.
He sends His traders in all directions:
He is the eternal Wholesaler.

Make your heart an ox, your mind a road:
Fill your sack with holy wisdom.
Kabir says, "Listen, O you sages,
my wares have reached their destination."

3

Hey, barmaid, hey, public woman,
hey foolish understanding,
I am straightening out my heart.
Mount Meru is my furnace
from which I draw streams of ambrosia—
my soul is drunk.

O my brothers, shout "Ram."
Drink, O sages—
for this wine is rare
and your thirst will be quenched. (Rest)

In fear is love.
The few who understand,
O my brothers,
taste the very essence of Hari.
There is ambrosia in everybody—
but only they whom He likes drink it.

One city: Nine gates.
Hold back your heart.
All worries vanish,
and the tenth gate opens:
My soul is drunk,
O my brothers.

I have no fears; suffering is at an end:
My soul is drunk, O my brothers.
Kabir speaks with authority:
"I obtained the liquor
by climbing the high mountain—
just like the grape's yeasty juice."

4

Steeped in lust, anger, desire,
you never understood His reality.
Your eyes have popped,
you can't see anything:
You've drowned without water.

Why do you strut, strut, strut?
You're only skin and bones,
with bad odors besides. (Rest)

You do not remember Ram.
Why go on deluding yourself:

Death is not too far away.
With great care you pamper your body —
it will only last a lifetime.

Nothing will come of all that you do.
What can mortals do, really?
If it pleases Him,
you will meet the True Guru,
and utter His one name.

In a little sand house
live these children of flesh.
Kabir, say,
"If Ram is forgotten,
even the most clever will drown."

5

A slanted turban,
a dainty strut:
You begin to chew a betel leaf.
"Love? Devotion?
I have things to do at court."

In your pride, you have forgotten Ram:
Gold, exquisitely beautiful women —
these you see as truth. (Rest)

Greed, lies, evil, great pride —
in these you spent your entire life.
Kabir, say, "In the end,
Death comes
and grabs the fool."

6

After beating your drum for a while,
you had to leave.
Though you amassed so much

that you had to tie it in bundles
and bury it in the earth—
still, none of it went with you. (Rest)

Your wife sits weeping on the threshold,
your mother goes as far
as the outer door.
Friends and relatives only go
as far as the cremation ground:
The swan must fly away alone.

That son, that wealth,
that town, that city,
you shall never see again.
Kabir says,
"Why don't you think of Ram?
You are wasting your life."

From Raga Bhairo

1

Hari's name is my wealth.
You can't tie it
in a bundle,
and you can't sell it. (Rest)

His name is my field,
His name is my garden:
Your slave serves You
and asks for Your protection.

His name is my money,
His name is my capital:
Besides You,
I have no assets.

His name is my family,
His name is my brother.
His name is my friend:
You will support me to the end.

Those who remain detached,
despite wealth,
Kabir, say,
"I am their friend."

2

Naked you came,
naked you shall leave.
None can stay —
not raja, not sovereign.

Raja Ram is my nine treasures.
For you, however,
there is only love
of pleasure, women, wealth. (Rest)

But these never came with you,
and they shall not leave with you.
What use is having elephants
tied at your door?

The fortress at Lanka
was made of gold:
So what did the fool Ravana
take with him?

Kabir, say,
"Think of virtue:
Gamblers leave
with both hands empty."

3

Vile is Brahma, vile Indra;
vile is the sun, vile the moon.

Vile and dirty is this world.
Only limitless, boundless Hari is pure. (Rest)

Vile are the gods of the universe;
vile are night, day, and the months.

Vile is the pearl, vile the diamond;
vile are air, fire, and water.

Vile is Shiva-Shankara-Mahesha;
vile are holy men, ascetics, and hermits.

Vile are yogis, Shaivites, with their long matted hair;
vile are the body and soul.

Kabir, say, "Only those slaves
are acceptable, are pure, who know Ram."

4

Make your heart Mecca
and your body the Ka'aba.
Make consciousness
its primal guru.

Hey, mullah, give the call for prayers:
One mosque, ten doors. (Rest)

Do away with sacrifice,
doubt and inner filth.
Make patience
your five daily prayers.

The Master of Hindus and Turks
is one and the same.
What use is being
a mullah or sheikh?

Kabir, say,
"I have become insane.
Slowly, slowly my heart
has blended with the Infinite."

5

A stream vanishes in the Ganges:
That stream ends up being the Ganges.

Kabir vanished when he shouted, "Ram":
I have become Truth; I need not wander. (Rest)

The tree vanishes into sandalwood:
That tree ends up being sandalwood.

Copper vanishes at the touch of the philosopher's stone:
That copper ends up being gold.

Kabir vanishes in the company of saints:
That Kabir ends up being Ram.

6

A *tilak* on your forehead,
a rosary in your hand,
vestments on your body:
People think Ram is a toy.

If I am mad,
then I am Yours, O Ram—
how can these people
know my secret? (Rest)

I do not pluck petals,
nor worship gods—
without devotion to Ram,
service is useless.

I worship the True Guru;
Him I ever wish to please.
For such service
I am granted solace at His court.

People say,
"Kabir's gone mad."
Only Ram knows
Kabir's secret.

7

When I turned around,
I forgot both family and caste:
My loom
is in the infinite Silence.

I have no quarrels:
I have given up on pundits and mullahs. (Rest)

I weave —
and I wear what I weave;
I sing
where I am not present.

I abandoned all
the written advice
given me by pundits and mullahs —
took none of it with me.

If love is in your heart
you can behold the Lord.
Those who found Him did so
by first finding themselves, O Kabir.

8

No one respects a poor man;
he may do a thousand things,
but no one pays any attention. (Rest)

If a poor man goes to a rich man,
the rich man does not even
look up at him.

If a rich man goes to a poor man,
he is respected —
and called "Sir."

The rich man and the poor man
are both brothers:
Prabhu's creation cannot be effaced.

Kabir, say, "Poor is he
who does not have
His name in his heart."

9

Serve the Guru and be devoted:
Put human birth to good use.
Even gods yearn for human shape—
serve Hari through this body.

Praise Gobind. Forget Him not:
That's the advantage of human birth. (Rest)

Before old age stains you,
before death clutches your body,
before your tongue stutters,
praise, O my soul, Sarangpani.

Worship him now, not later, O my brother.
The end comes—you can't do it then.
Now is the time for everything—
or you'll regret not crossing over.

He teaches service to His slaves:
And so they find Niranjan Deva.
Meet the Guru, and the gates will open:
You shall never be in the womb again.

Now is your chance. Now it's your turn.
Look inside your heart and meditate.
Kabir says, "Whether you win or lose,
I called out, I called out to you so many times."

10

Real wisdom is Shiva's city.
Gather there and meditate.
You will understand this life and the next;
no one dies in self-pride there.

I am thinking about my abode there:
Raja Ram is my theology. (Rest)

By the Source's root is my abode:
I place the moon above the sun.
The sun is fiery by the western door;
the Meru-sceptred One is above me.

The western door has a threshold;
above the threshold is a window.
Above the window is the tenth door.
Kabir, say, "It has no limits, no boundaries."

11

The true mullah battles his heart,
fights with death, as shown by his guru,
and stamps out Yama's pride.
My salaams to such a mullah.

Reverend sir,
you say He is so distant.
Why don't you calm your lusts
and find the Beautiful One. (Rest)

The true qazi searches his heart,
illumines his body with Brahma's fire,
and does not ejaculate even in his dreams.
Such a qazi will not grow old and die.

The true sultan draws two arrows,
holds in whatever wants out,
and gathers his legions in the sky's circle.
Such a sultan will have an umbrella of state over his head.

The yogi says, "Gorakh, Gorakh";
a Hindu takes the name of Rama;
a Muslim has the one Khuda:
Kabir's Swami is all-pervasive.

12

(by Guru Arjan Dev)

Those who call stones gods
waste their devotion.
Those who prostrate themselves
before stones
waste their efforts.

My Thakur is alive.
Prabhu bestows blessings on all. (Rest)

The blind do not see Deva,
who is inside them;
caught in illusion, they are trapped:
The silent stones do not speak.
Serving them bears no fruit.

If you rub sandal paste
on a corpse, tell me,
what good will it be to the corpse?
And if you roll a corpse in filth,
does it really matter to the corpse?

Kabir says, "I am shouting:
See and judge, O hardened fools,
those others have destroyed many homes.
Only Ram's lovers
are truly happy."

13

Fish in water are pierced by Maya;
moths around lamps are threaded by Maya.
Maya pricks an elephant with lust;
snakes, bumblebees are engulfed by Maya.

Maya is so enchanting, O my brother,
that she makes all living things stagger. (Rest)

Birds, beasts teem with Maya;
sugar vexes the fly.
Horses, camels are bridled by Maya;
the eighty-four *siddhas* are Maya's sport.

The six *jatis* are Maya's slaves,
as are the nine *nathas,* the sun, the moon.
Ascetics, great *rishis* are groomed by Maya;
death, the five angels are ruled by Maya.

Dogs, jackals are goaded by Maya;
so are monkeys, cheetahs, lions,
cats, sheep, foxes.
Trees and roots obey Maya.

Gods are drenched in Maya,
and so are oceans, sky, earth.
Kabir, say, "Maya governs those with their bellies.
Find the Sadhu, and break free."

14

As long as you say, "Mine, mine,"
you'll never succeed at anything.
When you stop saying, "Mine, mine,"
Prabhu will come and correct everything.

Ponder upon this wisdom, O my heart.
Why don't you think of Hari,
the destroyer of pain. (Rest)

As long as a lion lives in a forest,
that forest cannot burgeon.
When a jackal eats that lion,
the entire wood blossoms.

The victorious drown; the vanquished swim:
Their guru's grace bears them across.
The slave Kabir speaks that you may understand:
Love only Ram.

15

He has seven thousand angels,
a hundred thousand prophets,
eighty-eight million sheikhs,
and fifty-six million legions.

Who will listen to poor me?
His court is far away.
How will I find
His palace? (Rest)

He has thirty-three million house-servants;
eighty-four thousand wander like nomads.
He looked with favor on Father Adam—
but even Adam enjoyed paradise only for a while.

Those who abandon the scriptures and do satanic deeds,
have turmoil in their hearts, and their faces
are pale. They blame the world and fume against everyone:
They reap what they sow.

You are the Giver, and I, forever a beggar.
If I say no to You, I sin.
The slave Kabir asks for Your protection:
Keep me close to You, O Rahman.

16

Everyone says, "I am going there."
But I don't know where heaven is. (Rest)

They don't even know their own secret;
their heaven is in words only.

As long as your heart longs for heaven,
you cannot abide at His feet.

Moat? Fortress? City? City walls?
I don't even know the road to heaven.

Kabir, say, "What else can I say?
The company of saints is heaven."

17

How do you conquer this solid fort,
O my brother? It has two walls, three moats. (Rest)

Inside are the Five, the Twenty-five,
along with worldly love, pride, and malice.
Their commander is the great Maya herself.
I am a poor man, completely powerless.
What should I do, O Raghurai?

Lust is the door-keeper,
pain and solace sentinals,
sin and good deeds the gates.
Wrath is captain, the great quarreler—
and the rebel raja is the heart.

Pleasure is their coat of mail,
self-pride, their helmet,
falsehood, their taut bow.
Desire, which dwells in the heart,
is their arrow. This fort cannot be taken.

But love is my gun-cotton,
understanding my cannon.
I fire the ball of wisdom.
Carefully I lit the fire of Brahma—
and took the fort with only one shot.

With truth and patience beside me,
I began the fight,
and broke open both the doors.
By the grace of the saints and my guru,
I captured the rebel raja.

With the crowd of Krishna's sages,
and the might of meditation,
I cut the horrid noose of death.
The slave Kabir has scaled the fort
and taken up the reign that never ends.

18

Tying up Kabir in chains, they took him
to the deep, fathomless mother Ganges.

My heart did not sink, my body did not tremble,
my soul was absorbed in His lotus-like feet. (Rest)

The current of the Ganges broke my chains:
Kabir now sits on a deer-skin.

Kabir, say, "I had no friends nor companions:
Raghunath is my keeper, both in water and on land."

19

The Remote, the Inaccessible
makes a fort for His dwelling,
which He illumines with His light.
Lightning flashes—there is bliss
where the child Prabhu-Gobind plays.

My soul loves Ram's name:
Old age, death, doubt flee. (Rest)

They who care about castes
are forever singing praises about themselves.
But sweet melodies play unstruck
where the Lord Prabhu-Gopal dwells.

The remote, unknowable One,
who established the earth, the spheres,
the three worlds, and the three virtues,
lives in every heart: None knows Dharnidhar's secrets.

He reveals Himself in the blossom's fragrance.
He dwells in the nectar of a mud-flower.
His mantra is in the twelve-petalled heart,
where the Lord Kamlakant dwells.

His light is visible above and below;
He illumines the infinite sphere of silence:
Neither sun nor moon are found there;
the primal Niranjan enjoys Himself.

He knows the universe and each heart.
He bathes in Lake Mansarowar.
His mantra is, "I am He";
He is not concerned with good deeds or bad.

He has no caste, nor is he casteless;
He knows neither pain nor solace. He is in
the guru's house. He cannot be avoided.
He knows not birth or death: He is infinite silence.

Those who search for Him in their hearts,
and speak His words, will become Him.
They who place His mantra of light in their hearts,
Kabir, say, "Those mortals will certainly swim across."

20

Ten million suns shine for Him;
He has ten million Shivas and their Kailash paradises.
Ten million Durgas massage His feet;
ten million Brahmas recite the Vedas.

Whenever I beg, I beg from Ram:
I have nothing to do with the other gods. (Rest)

Ten million moons are His lamps;
He feeds three hundred and thirty million gods.
Ninety million planets stand in His court;
ten million Dharmrajas are His porters.

Ten million winds fan His summer-house;
ten million Sheshnagas draw His bed.
Ten million oceans are His water-carriers;
ten million forests are His hair.

Ten million Kuberas fill His treasuries;
ten million Lakshmis adorn themselves for him.
Ten million good and bad deeds await Him;
ten million Indras serve Him.

Fifty-six million clouds are His messengers:
They flash above each and every city.
Horrid black goddesses with dishevelled hair
and ten million Kalkas play before Gopal.

Ten million worlds are within His court;
ten million celestial musicians sing His praise.
Ten million wisdoms describe Parbrahma's virtues—
but still they cannot reach the end.

Fifty-five million Vamanas and those
who defeated Ravana's army form His hair.
He has ten million of those,
who, in the Puranas, humbled Duryodhana.

Ten million Kamas, who conquer the heart,
cannot equal Him. Kabir, say,
"Listen, O Sarangpani:
give me fearlessness—the only gift I beg for."

From Raga Basant

1

The earth bursts forth,
the sky blossoms;
each heart flowers
with Atma's light.

Raja Ram blossoms in such variety;
wherever I look, He is there. (Rest)

The four Vedas
sprout up
along with the Smriti
and the Western holy books.

Shankara who practices yoga
blooms full;
Kabir's Swami
is everywhere.

2

Pundits are drunk with the Puranas;
yogis are drunk with yoga.
Anchorites are drunk with pride;
ascetics are drunk with holy secrets.

All are drunk with pride, none is sober,
while thieves rob and pillage. (Rest)

Sukhdeva and Akrura were sober;
even the monkey-tailed Hanuman was sober.
Shankara was sober when serving Him.
In this Kalyuga age, Namdev and Jaidev are sober.

241

Many are the ways of being drunk or sober:
Being sober with your guru's words is best.
This body has many things to do;
Kabir, say, "Praise the name of Ram."

3

The wife gives birth to her husband;
the child bounces
his father on his knee.
The breastless woman gives suck.

O people, behold the ways of the present Age:
The son marries his own mother. (Rest)

The man with no feet jumps;
the mouthless man howls with laughter.
A man slumbers without sleeping;
milk is churned without a churn.

The udderless cow gives milk;
the long journey is taken without a road.
The way can't be found without the True Guru—
Kabir speaks so that you may understand.

4

When Prahlada went to school,
he took many
little friends with him.
"Why are you teaching me
this and that?
Write on my slate, 'Lord Gopal.' "

"O sir, I will not let go of Ram's name.
I don't want to study anything else." (Rest)

Sanda and Marka went home and told on him;
Prahlada was told to come at once.
"Forget about Ram.

I'll let go of you only
when you promise to do
what I tell you."

"Why do you harass me?
How can I forget that Prabhu who made
water, land, hills, and mountains?
It would be like swearing at my guru.
You can do what you like with me:
Kill me, burn me."

In anger, the father drew out his broadsword:
"Tell me, where is your Savior now?"
And the god emerged from a pillar
in a terrifying incarnation,
and flayed Harnakhasa
with His claws.

That was the Primal Being,
the God of gods;
for the love of His devotee
He assumed the guise of Narsingha.
Kabir, say, "None knows of His powers:
He saved Prahlada many, many times."

5

In this body and soul lives the thief, Madana,
who has stolen my gem of divine wisdom.
Prabhu, I have no master; to whom can I complain?
He has robbed so many others.
What's so special about me?

O Madho, I can't bear all this pain.
What can my weak heart do? (Rest)

Sanaka, Sanandana, Shiva, Sukhdeva, Brahma,
and all others born from the navel of the lotus,
poets, devotees, and matted-haired yogis—
all lived their various lives
and left.

You are fathomless. I cannot know Your depth.
O Prabhu-Dinanatha, to whom can I complain?
Take away all my sorrows.
Kabir sings the virtues
of the Sea of solace.

6

One merchant, five shopkeepers,
twenty-five oxen. Nine staffs,
ten sacks, tied by seventy-two ropes:
This contract cannot last.

I don't need this business, which eats away
all my principle and increases my interest. (Rest)

My business is weaving the seven threads,
twining in deeds done in this world.
The three tax-collectors argue:
The trader leaves empty-handed.

The assets are taken, the business dissolves:
Scattered is the caravan. Kabir, say, "O my heart,
your business will flourish and your doubts will flee
when you become absorbed into the infinite Silence."

From Raga Basant-Hindola

7

Unholy was your mother,
unholy your father,
unholy was all
their fruit.
They were born unholy,
and luckless;
they went and died unholy.

Say, pundit, which place is really holy,
where I can sit and eat my food? (Rest)

Unholy is the tongue,
unholy is speech,
unholy are ears and eyes.
You can't rid the senses
of their unholiness,
O you who burn with the fire
of being Brahmins.

Unholy is fire,
unholy is water,
unholy, your kitchen.
Unholy is the ladle
with which you serve food;
unholy are those
who sit and eat.

Unholy is dung,
unholy the cooking square,
unholy its boundaries.
Kabir, say,
"Only they are holy
who understand
truth."

From Raga Basant

8

You walk gently like a cow;
your tail-hair glistens.

You're in the house now,
eat what you can find: Why go elsewhere? (Rest)

You lick the hand-mill and eat the flour.
Where are you taking that mill wiping rag?

Now you're eyeing that pot;
you'll get a stick or a club across the back.

Kabir, say, "You've eaten quite well;
take care: A brick or stone may brain you."

From Raga Sarang

1

O man, why are you proud of so little:
Eight hundred pounds of flour,
a bit of money in your purse,
and such a swaggering walk. (Rest)

And if you gain greater renown—
a hundred villages, with many thousands
in revenues—you'll still be master
for a few days only, like leaves in a forest.

No one ever brought wealth with him,
nor took it with him—
kings greater than Ravana
vanished in a trice.

Honor Hari's sages:
They repeat His name and live forever.
They, to whom Gobind shows mercy,
meet the crowd of saints.

Mother, father, wife, son
will not go with you in the end.
Kabir says, "Praise Hari, O fool,
so your life won't be wasted."

2

Rajashram, I never realized Your reality;
I am the handmaid of Your saints. (Rest)

They go laughing, who come weeping;
they go weeping, who come laughing.
Habitations become deserts;
deserts become habitations.

Water is made land, land into wells,
wells into mountains.
Those on earth are raised to the sky;
those in the sky are cast down.

A beggar becomes a raja;
a raja becomes a beggar.
A fool becomes a wise pundit;
a wise pundit becomes a fool.

Men emerge from women;
women emerge from men.
Kabir, say, "I immolate myself
for the Beloved of the sages."

3

Who but Hari
is my soul's support?
Mother, father,
brother, son, wife—
their love lasts
for a little while only. (Rest)

Make a raft
for what lies ahead:
You can't rely on wealth,
and you can't rely
on this clay-pot—it might shatter.

Ask for dust from saints' feet
and you will be rewarded
for your religion and good works.
Kabir, say, "Listen, O you sages,
this heart is like a bird in the forest—
it might fly away."

From Raga Parbhati

1

From Raga Vibhas-Parbhati

Gone is my fear of death and rebirth:
He has shown me solace in His own time.

Light awakens; darkness is erased.
Meditation has given me Ram's gem. (Rest)

Bliss reigns, sorrow is so distant:
The heart encloses the jewel of love.

Whatever happened, happened because of You:
Those who realize this blend with the Infinite.

Kabir says, "Sin is humbled:
My heart has merged with Jagjivan."

2

If Allah lives in a mosque,
to whom belongs the rest of the land?
Hindus say His name dwells in an idol:
I see the truth in neither.

Allah, Ram, I live by Your name.
Be merciful, O Sain. (Rest)

The south is Hari's abode; Allah's camp
is in the west. Look inside your own heart—
inside your heart of hearts—
there is His abode, His camp.

251

Brahmins fast twice a month twenty-four times;
qazis fast in the month of Ramadan:
Neglecting the remaining eleven months,
they search for treasure in one month.

Why go and bathe in Orissa?
Why bow heads in a mosque?
You're a thug at heart.
Why pray and go on a *hajj* to the Ka'aba.

All these men and women—
they are Your forms.
Kabir is the infant of Ram-Allah;
everyone is my guru, my *pir*.

Kabir says, "Listen, O men and women,
seek only one shelter:
Repeat His name, O mortals.
Only then will you swim across."

3

In the beginning
was Allah's radiance;
all men are His creation.
From this radiance was born the Word—
who can ever turn good into evil?

O mortals, O my brothers,
do not be mistaken:
The Creator is in the creation;
the creation is in the Creator.
He is everywhere. (Rest)

From the same clay
the Shaper
shaped many things:
The flaw is in the clay-pots,
not in the Potter.

The sole True One is in everything;
everything is His creation.
Only they who recognize His command,
and know Him to be the true One
will be called His slaves.

The indescribable Allah
is beyond words:
The Guru has handed out sugar.
Kabir says, "My doubt has vanished:
I see Niranjan in all."

4

Don't say the Vedas, the Western holy books are lies —
liars are they who do not ponder upon them.
If you say that Khuda is in everything,
then why do you kill chickens?

O mullah, do you call this Khuda's justice?
The doubt in your heart can never vanish. (Rest)

You grab a living creature, kill its body,
and then bless the remains.
Its light blends with the indestructible Light —
what have you really made *halal*?

Why purify yourself? Why wash your mouth?
Why bend your head in the mosque?
If there is malice in your heart,
why do you go to the Ka'aba?

You are unholy. You can never know the Holy One:
You do not know His secret.
Kabir says, "Now that you've lost heaven,
you make yourself content with hell."

5

Silence is Your evening prayer,
O Deva, O Treasure of light,
O Master, O primal One,

O All-pervasive.
Despite their intense meditation,
saints could never find Your limits—
yet they stayed close
to Your protection.

Accept this final devotion,
O Purukh-Niranjan.
Worship the True Guru,
O my brothers.
Brahma stands and meditates
upon the Vedas:
The Indescribable
remains undescribed.

Make truth your oil,
His name your wick,
and illumine
your body.
The lamp is lit
by Jagdish:
Only a wise man
can guess the secret.

All kinds
of instruments play,
though they are untouched:
Sarangpani is everywhere.
The slave Kabir
performs the final devotion for you,
O unmoveable Niranjan.

The Slokas of Kabir

1

The Slokas of Kabir

Kabir,
Ram on my tongue
is my rosary.
From the beginning of the ages,
it has brought solace
to all devotees.

2

Kabir,
Everyone laughs at my caste;
but I honor it:
It was in this caste
that I got to worship Sirjanhar.

3

Kabir,
why do you vacillate?
Why is your heart uncertain?
He is the Lord of all solace.
Drink the essence
of Ram's name.

4

Kabir,
these gold earrings
set with rubies
are like burnt reeds,
if His name is not
in your heart.

5

Kabir,
few die while still alive;
they sing His praises
without fear.
Wherever I look,
He is there.

6

Kabir,
on the day I die,
there will be much rejoicing:
I shall meet my Prabhu,
and my friends
will praise Gobind.

7

Kabir,
I am the worst of all;
all are good except me.
Those who have realized
the same thing
are my friends.

8

Kabir,
she came to me
in so many disguises.
Each time,
my guru saved me—
and she bowed to me
and left.

9

Kabir,
kill her at whose death
all will rejoice.
All will say "Well-done";
no one will think it bad.

10

Kabir,
on darkest of nights,
thieves awake.
They sneak about
with nooses:
They are damned
by Bhagwan.

11

Kabir,
beautiful is that little
sandalwood sapling,
ringed by forest trees which bear bright flowers
but are useless:
They take on
the sandal's fragrance
just by being near it.

12

Kabir,
a bamboo is hollow,
despite being tall.
It may grow beside a sandalwood-tree,
but it can never
be fragrant.

13

Kabir,
for the sake of the world,
you lost your faith —
but the world would not go
with you in the end.
You axed your own feet.

14

Kabir,
wherever I went
I saw colorful spectacles:
In my opinion the world
is a desert
without Ram's love.

15

Kabir,
blessed is a saint's hovel;
the city of the false
is a furnace.
The palace
that has not Hari's name
may burn
for all I care.

16

Kabir,
why weep
when sages die?
They have gone home.
Weep rather
for the poor slave,
sold from shop to shop.

17

Kabir,
a godless man
is like food cooked with garlic—
though it is eaten
in a far corner,
you smell it sooner or later.

18

Kabir,
Maya is a pot full of milk,
breath is the churn.
Sages eat the butter,
the world gets the whey.

19

Kabir,
Maya is a pot full of milk,
breath the pouring iced-water.
Those who churn well
eat the butter;
others are still churning.

20

Kabir,
Maya is a thief
secretly plundering the shop.
Only Kabir is not robbed:
He cut her up
into little pieces.

21

Kabir,
you can't be happy
in this world
just by having many friends.
Those who think of the One
have everlasting solace.

22

Kabir,
the world is scared of dying;
I'm thrilled by it—
only by dying do you find
supreme eternal bliss.

23

Kabir,
now that you've secured
Ram's essence,
do not untie the knot:
There is no city,
no appraiser,
no buyers, no price.

24

Kabir,
love those
whose master is Ram.
Pundits, rajas, sovereigns—
what use are they?

25

Kabir,
when you love the One,
all fear flees—
it doesn't matter
whether you grow
your hair long,
or shave it off.

26

Kabir,
the world
is a grime-covered house:

The blind live in it.
I honor those who went in
and came right out again.

27

Kabir,
this body has to go,
but try to keep it safe.
Those who had millions
all left barefoot.

28

Kabir,
this body must go,
but try to lead it
to that road
where it can meet saints
and sing Hari's praise.

29

Kabir,
the whole world will die—
but no one knows why.
Die in such a way
that you may not
have to die again.

30

Kabir,
human birth is hard to get:
You won't get it again and again,
as in the forest,
the ripe fruit falls
to the earth
and can never be put
on the branch again.

31

Kabir,
You alone are Kabir;
only Your name is Kabir.
Ram's gem is found only
when this body is forgotten.

32

Kabir,
don't grumble;
you won't get what you want:
None can erase
the deeds of Allah-Karim.

33

Kabir, the false
will be found out
on Ram's touchstone.
Only those who die
while still alive
will pass Ram's test.

34

Kabir,
those who wear sumptuous clothes,
and eat dainty things,
yet know not Hari's name,
will be taken
to Yama's city in fetters.

35

Kabir,
this raft is ancient—
it has sprung a thousand leaks.
Those travelling light

swam away—
those with great loads
drowned.

36

Kabir,
bones burn like wood,
hair burns like grass.
Seeing this world burn,
I, Kabir,
am saddened.

37

Kabir,
why be proud of bones
wrapped around with skin.
Those who rode
on choicest of horses
under umbrellas
once again are dust.

38

Kabir,
don't be proud
of your high palace.
Today or tomorrow
you will lie in the earth,
with grass sprouting above.

39

Kabir,
don't be proud.
Don't laugh at the poor.
Your boat is still
on the sea;
who knows
what will happen.

40

Kabir,
don't pride yourself
on your exquisite body.
Today or tomorrow
you'll leave it behind,
like a snake sloughing its skin.

41

Kabir,
loot—
if loot you must—
now that Ram's name
is being looted.
Later, you'll be sorry,
when breath leaves you.

42

Kabir,
no one burns
his own house,
including all his five sons,
and then proceeds to love Ram.

43

Is there any one
who will sell his son?
Is there anyone
who will sell his daughter?
Kabir wants to go
into partnership with them,
and carry on a trade with Hari.

44

Kabir,
remember—
don't forget—

all your past pleasures
are worth no more
than a pinch of sugar.

45

Kabir,
once I thought
that knowledge was good,
and then that being joyful
was better than learning.
But now I forsake not Ram's service—
no matter what people say.

46

Kabir,
how can men
who have no understanding
in their hearts abuse me?
Kabir meditates on Ram;
he has given up
all other things.

47

Kabir,
the foreigner's coat
is enveloped by fire;
his cloak is burnt
to ash—
but the thread holding it together
has not even felt the heat.

48

Kabir,
the cloak is burnt to ash,
the skull bursts into chips.
The poor yogi played for a day:
Dust now covers the place
where he sat and meditated.

49

Kabir,
the fish is in the pond.
The fisherman
casts his net—
leave this pond,
O fish,
and seek the protection
of the wide sea.

50

Kabir, don't leave the sea,
though it be bitter
with brine.
Seeking out little ponds
is not good.

51

Kabir,
the rafts without owners
were swept away—
they had no boatmen.
Practise poverty and meekness,
no matter what happens.

52

Kabir,
the devotee's bitch is better
than the mother
of a godless man.
The one ever hears Hari's name and praise,
the other only
deals in sin.

53

Kabir,
lean is the stag;

this lake is circled
by green trees.
There are thousands of hunters.
He is alone—
how can he survive?

54

Kabir,
they who make their home
on the banks of the Ganges
can drink holy water—
but without devotion to Hari,
they cannot be saved.
Saying this,
Kabir meditates.

55

Kabir,
my mind has become holy
like the water of the Ganges.
Hari follows me around,
calling out, "Kabir, Kabir."

56

Kabir,
saffron is yellow
and lime, white.
You meet the beloved Ram
when both these colors
fade away.

57

Kabir,
when saffron
is yellow no longer,
and lime no longer white,
then love erases

caste, family, tribe—
for such love
I am ready to die.

58

Kabir,
narrow is the door
to salvation:
A tenth part of a mustard seed.
And my heart
is an elephant—
how can it pass through?

59

Kabir,
may I meet that true guru
who in his mercy
will open wide
the door of salvation,
so I can easily enter in.

60

Kabir,
I have neither shed nor hut,
neither a house nor a village.
Hari, don't ask who I am:
I have neither caste nor name.

61

Kabir,
I want to die—
but let it be
at Hari's door.
And perhaps Hari will say,
"Who is that lying at my door."

62

Kabir,
I didn't do it,
nor ever could;
my body could not do it either.
I don't know what Hari did —
but it became Kabir, Kabir.

63

Kabir,
if in his dreams
a sleeping man utters, "Ram,"
let my skin
become shoe-leather
for his feet.

64

Kabir,
we are clay dolls
named "humans";
although guests for a few days,
we try to gather
so much.

65

Kabir,
with great pain
I finely grind henna;
yet You never even spoke to me,
nor put the henna
on Your feet.

66

Kabir,
how can I leave that door

from which no one
drives you away
once you've arrived there?

67

Kabir,
I was going to drown,
but waves of virtue
pushed me on to shore:
I had jumped into the water
when I saw that my raft
was leaking.

68

Kabir,
a sinner doesn't like devotion,
nor does he like to worship Hari.
A fly avoids sandalwood,
and hurries towards stench.

69

Kabir,
the physician died,
the patient died,
the whole wide world died.
Only Kabir did not die,
for whom
there were no mourners.

70

Kabir,
those who do not worship Ram
are hollow inside.
The body
is like a wooden pot:
You can't put it
on top of the fire.

71

Kabir,
my heart is pleased.
Why fear death?
In Your hand
is the vermilion-filled coconut.

72

Kabir,
the sugarcane suffers
when you peel it,
chew it, and suck out its juice.
This is how you should suffer
and die for virtue:
No one calls an evil man good.

73

Kabir,
you fill a clay-pot with water;
today or tomorrow it will crack.
If you remember not your Guru,
you'll be robbed
right in the middle of things.

74

Kabir,
I'm Ram's dog,
and Motia is my name.
There's a chain around my neck,
and wherever He pulls,
there I go.

75

Kabir,
why do you show off
your wooden rosary to people?

If your heart
doesn't remember Ram,
what good is a rosary?

76

Kabir,
separation from the Beloved
coils around my heart
like a snake.
No mantras work.
I cannot live without Ram.
If I go on living,
I'll go mad.

77

Kabir,
the philosopher's stone
and sandalwood
have the same properties:
By touching them
iron and plain wood
turn into the best.

78

Kabir,
Yama's blow is vicious.
I can't bear it.
I have met a Sadhu
who will let me
hold on to His sleeve.

79

Kabir,
the physician says,
"I am the best;
I know all there is to know
about medicine."

But that belongs to Gopal;
He can snatch it all away
whenever He wants.

80

Kabir,
take and beat your drum
for a few days:
Passengers crossing a river
meet in the boat,
and then never
see each other
again.

81

Kabir,
if I make ink
out of all the oceans,
and pens out of all
the forests,
and make the earth my paper—
I still could never finish
writing the praises of Hari.

82

Kabir,
there's nothing wrong
with being a weaver by caste—
Gopal lives in my heart.
Ram meets
and embraces Kabir:
All the snares disappear.

83

Kabir,
no one burns down
his own house,

kills his five sons,
and then proceeds to love Ram.

84

Kabir,
no one would burn down
his own house.
The blind don't understand,
though Kabir
keeps yelling out to them.

85

Kabir,
the suttee climbs
on to the pyre:
"O cremation-ground,
you now are my friend.
Listen:
You are all I have left—
it is now
I need you most."

86

Kabir,
my heart is a bird
that flits and flies everywhere.
Whatever company he meets,
he eats their fruit.

87

Kabir,
you have found the place
you were looking for.
You have become Him
whom you thought different
from you.

88

Kabir,
I am being destroyed
by evil friends,
like a banana-tree beside
a wild caper-tree.
Whenever the caper sways,
it tears the banana-tree:
Don't go near it.

89

Kabir,
your head is burdened
by other men's sins—
but still you don't mind.
Aren't you worried about your own load?
The road ahead
is treacherous.

90

Kabir,
the charcoaled wood
in the forest
cried out where it lay,
"I do not want a blacksmith
to come and cart me away:
He will burn me
a second time."

91

Kabir,
with the death of one,
two died.
With the death of two,
four died.
With the death of four,
six died:
four males and two females.

92

Kabir,
I searched the whole world,
but found no resting place.
You who have not thought
about Hari's name,
why do you roam around?

93

Kabir,
keep company with the sages;
they will stay with you till the end.
Don't associate
with the godless;
they will destroy you.

94

Kabir,
some, while in the world,
meditate upon Him—
who is all-pervasive.
Others never think of Hari's name—
they will be reborn again.

95

Kabir,
hope in Ram:
You'll be disappointed
if you rely on others.
Those who forsake Hari
will go to hell.

96

Kabir,
I made many followers and disciples,
yet never made Keshava my friend.

I started out
to meet Hari,
but my heart got diverted halfway there.

97

Kabir,
what can a poor man do
if Ram will not support him:
Each branch
that I place my foot on
breaks beneath me.

98

Kabir,
those who preach to others,
will get sand in their mouths.
They look after other people's harvests,
while their own
rots away.

99

Kabir,
befriend sages,
though you have to eat husks.
Come what may, do not
fall into the company
of the godless.

100

Kabir,
among sages,
His love doubles day by day.
The godless are like black blankets:
No matter how much you wash them,
they'll never be white.

101

Kabir,
you didn't shave your soul,
so why shave your head?
All things are done
through the heart:
Shaving the head
is useless.

102

Kabir,
forget not Ram's name;
let body and wealth go,
if they must.
Dedicate your heart
to His flower-like feet,
and be absorbed in Ram's name.

103

Kabir,
of the lyre that I play,
all the strings are broken.
What can the poor lyre do—
the player himself
went away long ago.

104

Kabir,
shave the head of that guru's mother
who does not dispel doubt:
He himself drowns
with the four Vedas,
and all his disciples
are swept away.

105

Kabir,
you hide all the sins
that you commit
away in your heart.
But in the end
when Dharmraja enquires,
they'll all be revealed.

106

Kabir,
you forgot about Hari
and became busy
raising your family;
immersed in work,
you never noticed
that brothers and family
were gone.

107

Kabir,
forsaking Hari,
a woman goes
to a wake at night;
she will be reborn
as a she-snake,
who eats her own children.

108

Kabir,
the woman who forgets Hari
and fasts in honor of Hoi
shall be reborn
as a donkey, laden
with hundreds of pounds.

109

Kabir,
remembering Hari in your heart
is the greatest of wisdoms:
if you play on stilts
and then fall—
there's little hope.

110

Kabir,
blessed is the mouth
that says, "Ram."
Not only the poor body,
but the whole village
will become holy
because of it.

111

Kabir,
blessed is the family
in which a servant of Hari is born.
The family that has no such servant
is like a useless forest tree.

112

Kabir,
riding countless horses and elephants,
with thousands of banners waving—
better far than these pleasures
is to beg for food,
so that you can pass your days
remembering Hari.

113

Kabir,
I have wandered over all the earth,
with my drum slung over my shoulder.

I played and tested other drums—
but found none
I could call my own.

114

Once,
pearls were scattered on a road,
and a blind man
happened by:
Without Jagdish's light,
the whole world
kept passing by.

115

Kabir's family drowned
when this brilliant son
was born:
Forgetting Hari,
he brought home wealth.

116

Kabir,
if you go to see a sage
take no one with you.
Don't turn back.
Keep going—
no matter what.

117

Kabir,
the world is chained.
Don't get yourself
tied down, too, O Kabir.
As salt is lost in flour,
so will this golden body
be lost.

118

Kabir,
the swan is about to fly away;
the body will soon be buried.
He can only speak
through signs now—
but still
the greed in his eyes doesn't fade.

119

Kabir,
may I see You with my eyes,
hear Your name
with my own ears.
Speak Your name
in my words, O Lord;
rest Your flower-like feet
on my heart.

120

Kabir,
by the guru's grace,
I have been saved
from heaven and hell.
I have been absorbed forever
into the joy
of His lotus-like feet.

121

Kabir,
how can I measure the joy
that eminates from His flower-like feet?
Beauty is beyond words:
You have to see
to believe.

122

Kabir,
even if I saw Him,
how would I describe Him?
No one would be satisfied.
Hari is His own equal.
In gladness,
I sing His praise.

123

Kabir,
a crane pecks
and remembers her young;
pecks and pecks
and remembers her young.
Like her young to the crane,
so Maya is dear to the heart.

124

Kabir,
clouds spread across the sky.
Rain fills
lakes and ponds.
Those who yearn
like the *chatrik*-bird,
what misery they must suffer.

125

Kabir,
the *chakava*-bird,
separated from her beloved at night,
can meet him at dawn.
Those separated from Ram
can meet Him
neither day nor night.

126

Kabir,
they are separated
from the sea:
"O conch, stay in the sea,
or you will have to shriek horribly
in the house of the gods
at each sunrise."

127

Kabir,
what're you doing,
sleeping away?
Get up and weep for fear:
How can their sleep be sweet
who are buried deep in the graves?

128

Kabir,
what're you doing,
sleeping away?
Get up and worship Murari.
One day
you'll sleep all right,
with your knees
stretched out.

129

Kabir,
what're you doing,
sleeping away?
Get up. Stay awake.
Embrace Him
from whom you've been separated.

130

Kabir,
keep after those sages.
Stay on the road.
You'll be holy
when you see them;
and when you meet up with them
you'll repeat His name.

131

Kabir,
don't befriend the godless;
run away from them.
If you touch a sooty pot,
you're bound to blacken
your hand.

132

Kabir,
you never thought of Ram;
and now old age
has caught up with you.
The door of your house
is on fire —
what can you do now?

133

Kabir,
the road was made
by Kratar.
There is none other but Him.
Sirjanhar is unique.

134

Kabir,
fruit begins to appear,

mangoes ripen.
Their owner will get them,
if crows don't eat them first.

135

Kabir,
people buy idols,
and then worship them;
and they stubbornly go
to bathe in holy shrines.
They copy and imitate
what they see—
they wander about,
totally lost.

136

Kabir,
the world turns Parmeshwar
into stone
and then worships it.
Those who adhere
to this kind of religion
will drown
in the black river.

137

Kabir,
prisons of paper,
with gates of ink;
stones have drowned
the world,
and pundits
are robbers on the road.

138

Kabir,
do today

what you have to do tomorrow.
Do it this instant.
You won't be doing anything later
when Death comes
and stands over your head.

139

Kabir,
I see men shining like lacquer:
They look sharp, alert, and virtuous,
but in reality
they are senseless and unholy.

140

Kabir,
Yama can't fool me.
He who created
this little boy Yama—
that Parvidgar
is the one I worship.

141

Kabir,
He is musk.
All his slaves are bumblebees.
The more Kabir serves Him,
the more Ram lives in him.

142

Kabir,
you fall into the joys
of your family;
Ram is on the periphery.
And Dharmraja's legions
come running at you,
right in the middle
of your pomp and show.

143

Kabir,
a pig is better than a godless man—
at least it keeps the village clean.
But when the godless man dies
no one remembers even his name.

144

Kabir,
cowrie by cowrie,
you hoard thousands and millions.
When you leave
you get nothing—
even your underwear
is taken from you.

145

Kabir,
what would it matter
if I became a Vaishnava saint,
wearing four necklaces:
Purified gold outside—
but wax inside.

146

Kabir,
become like gravel on roads;
forsake all pride.
If you become such a slave,
only then will you meet Bhagwan.

147

Kabir,
if you became like gravel—
so what?
You'd just be a pain

to travellers.
Your slave should be like the dust
of the earth.

148

Kabir,
if you became like dust—
so what?
You'd only blow around
and settle on people.
The slave of Hari
should be like water,
which can take on any shape.

149

Kabir,
if you became like water—
so what?
You would be hot or cold.
We need a slave of Hari,
who is like Hari.

150

Kabir,
if you have a high palace,
with banners waving on top,
gold, and ravishing women—
far better it is
to beg for food
at every door and sing His praises
with the crowd of sages.

151

Kabir,
better than a flourishing city
is a desert where you can sit

and worship Ram.
The place without beloved Ram
is like the city of Yama.

152

Kabir,
where the Ganges and Jamuna meet,
where unchanging Silence abides —
there have I made my monastery,
the way to which
all the holy men seek.

153

Kabir,
the softness of a new seedling —
if it could be preserved forever —
a mere diamond, no,
a hundred million rubies
would not be price enough
for that softness.

154

Kabir,
I saw a strange thing:
A diamond was being sold in a shop —
but because no buyer would look at it,
it sold for a few cowries.

155

Kabir,
where there's divine wisdom,
there is righteousness;
where there's falsehood,
there is sin.
Where there's greed,
there is death.
Where there's mercy,
there is He.

156

Kabir,
if you forsake Maya—
so what?
You still haven't forsaken pride.
Munis, even the best of *munis,*
rotted away in their pride.
Pride devours all.

157

Kabir,
I met the True Guru—
his word struck me like an arrow.
I fell as soon as I was hit:
My heart was pierced.

158

Kabir,
what can the True Guru do
if His disciples are worthless?
Words have no effect on the blind—
like blowing into a green bamboo
to make a sound.

159

Kabir,
that wife of a king
who rides on horses and elephants
is not equal to the woman
who draws water
for Hari's slaves.

160

Kabir,
why abuse the king's wife?
Why honor Hari's handmaid?

The one adorns her hair
to arouse lust,
the other remembers Hari's name.

161

Kabir,
the truss became my support:
The True Guru gave me patience.
Kabir bought the diamond
on the banks of Lake Mansarowar.

162

Kabir,
Hari is the diamond,
which His servant the jeweller
displays in his shop.
As soon as a diamond merchant comes along,
its real worth will be known.

163

Kabir,
you call out to Ram
when you're in trouble—
remember Him in that way always:
This is how you will come to live
in the deathless City.
Hari replaces what you lose.

164

Kabir,
these two are necessary for devotion:
a sage and Ram.
Ram gives you salvation,
and a sage
makes you repeat His name.

165

Kabir,
a big crowd follows the road
walked by pundits.
Ram's road is a narrow slanting
mountain path,
which Kabir is walking.

166

Kabir,
you die worrying
about what other people will say—
and so you stick to family tradition.
Tell me, whose family is going to be ashamed
when they lay you out
on the cremation ground?

167

Kabir says,
"O wretched people,
you'll all drown,
caring about what other people think.
Whatever happens to your neighbor
will happen to you as well."

168

Kabir,
better to beg from house to house,
eating bread made from many flours:
you don't owe anyone anything—
large is the land,
large the realm.

169

Kabir,
possessions give you worries—

no possession, no worries.
Those who have no possessions
deem Indra a pauper.

170

Kabir,
the pond is full to the brim,
yet no one can drink the water.
But through good fortune,
you've found a way—
now drink, Kabir, drink great mouthfuls.

171

Kabir,
like stars that slip away at dawn,
so this body fades away.
The letters of His name
never fade away:
Kabir's holding them fast.

172

Kabir,
the wooden house is on fire.
All the pundits burned to death,
while all the fools got up
and ran away.

173

Kabir,
drive doubt far away—
put away all this paper.
Having gone through all the letters
of the alphabet,
place your thoughts
upon Hari's feet.

174

Kabir,
saints don't forsake sainthood,
though they meet millions
who aren't saints:
The sandal-bush,
growing on Malaya mountain,
though encircled by snakes,
does not lose its cooling touch.

175

Kabir,
my mind became free from passion,
when it obtained Brahma's wisdom.
The fire that burns the world
is like water to His slave.

176

Kabir,
all this is the Creator's;
few know it.
The Master,
or the slave at His court,
alone know.

177

Kabir,
blessed are those who fear Him:
They forget all else.
The rain fell on water,
and flowing away,
merged with the sea.

178

Kabir,
gathering together dust,

He tied it up like a packet:
It looks good for a few days—
but really it's only dust.

179

Kabir,
all bodies were created
so they would shine
like the sun or moon.
Without meeting the Guru-Gobind,
they again become dust.

180

Where there is wisdom,
there is fear.
Where there is fear,
there Hari is not.
Kabir speaks with great care:
O sages,
listen with your hearts.

181

Kabir,
those who never understood,
sleep peacefully.
I, who understand, am filled
with endless worries.

182

Kabir,
those who are being beaten
cry out each time they're hit.
When I was hit on the heart,
O Kabir, I remained standing.

183

Kabir,
a spear-thrust is nothing—
though stabbed you can still survive.
But they who can bear the Word's thrust
are great gurus,
and I am their slave.

184

Kabir says,
"O mullah, why do you climb up
to the minaret?
The Sain is not deaf, you know.
He for whom you're giving the call
is right inside your own heart.

185

O sheikh,
you have no inner peace—
so why go on a pilgrimage to the Ka'aba?
Kabir, how can they ever meet Khuda,
whose hearts
are not full of peace?

186

Kabir,
worship Allah.
Pain flees when you meditate upon Him.
The Sain will reveal Himself
in your heart. His name will put out
the raging fire.

187

Kabir,
force is cruelty—
though by using His name

they call it lawful.
When you have to settle accounts
in His office,
what will become of you then?

188

Kabir,
boiled rice with lentils,
seasoned with tasty salt,
is the best of foods:
I cannot slit throats
to have meat with my bread.

189

Kabir,
when the Guru touches you,
love for the world and all desires
that burn your body
will be quenched.
Joy and grief will not burn you.
Everywhere, you'll see Hari.

190

Kabir,
there's a secret in saying, "Ram."
This is what you have to know:
The people and the actors in a *Ras-Leela*
are talking about the same Ram.

191

Kabir,
say, "Ram, Ram."
But while doing so remember:
The One is found in all,
the other was in one body only.

192

Kabir,
the house in which saints and Hari
are not served
is like a cremation ground,
where demons dwell.

193

Kabir has become mute and mad.
His ears are deaf;
lame are his feet—
he was struck
by the Guru's arrow.

194

Kabir,
those hit by the Guru's arrow
fall to the ground at once—
their hearts pierced.

195

Kabir,
a pure drop fell from heaven
on the parched earth—
but it became like ash
in a furnace:
This is what happens
when there is no truth.

196

Kabir,
once the pure drop from heaven
blends and mixes with the earth,
no matter how clever you are,
you cannot separate it again.

197

Kabir,
I was on my way
to the Ka'aba for the *hajj*
when I met Khuda on the road.
The Sain got mad at me and said,
"Who told you to go there?"

198

Kabir,
so many times have I gone
to the Ka'aba on the *hajj*—
so many times, O Kabir.
O Sain, what have I done wrong?
O Pir, why don't you speak to me?

199

Kabir,
those who cruelly kill living creatures,
and then call it *halal*—
when they go to His office,
and He takes out their record,
what will be their fate?

200

Kabir,
using force is cruel—
you'll have to answer to Khuda.
When your record book is taken out,
you'll be slapped across the face.

201

Kabir,
those who have pure hearts
won't be worried about giving account.

In that court of truth
no one will drag them away
by the scruff of their necks.

202

Kabir says,
"Difficult are you to destroy
in heaven and earth, O Duality.
All the six types of ascetics,
and the eighty-four *siddhas*
are steeped in doubt."

203

Kabir says,
"Nothing is mine;
all that I have is Yours.
If I return all that belongs to You,
what would I have left?"

204

Kabir says,
"By saying, 'You, You,'
I have become You.
'I am' is in me no longer.
When the difference
between us was erased,
I saw You everywhere."

205

Kabir,
those who think only
of doing evil
and rely on false hope,
get up and leave forlorn,
with all their desires
unfulfilled.

206

Kabir,
those who ponder upon Hari
are full of solace in the world.
Those protected by Sirjanhar
don't roam around here and there.

207

Kabir,
I was being crushed
like seeds in an oil-press—
but the True Guru set me free.
Love, old as all my births,
flickered once again.

208

Kabir,
I kept putting it off every day—
and the interest-payments kept going up.
I never worshipped Hari,
I never tore up my account register—
and Death came walking along.

209

(by Guru Arjan Dev)

Kabir,
a barking dog always
runs after dead meat.
But, by His mercy,
I have found the True Guru
who has set me free.

210

(by Guru Arjan Dev)

Kabir,
the earth belongs to saints,
but thieves have gotten hold of it.
The earth does not feel their weight:
They do nothing
but gain.

211

(by Guru Arjan Dev)

Kabir,
you beat rice husks
with a mallet
to get at the grain.
Thus those who sit with evil men
will have to account for it
to Dharmraja.

212

"O Namdev,
I think you're ensnared
by worldly love," said his friend Trilochan,
"why are you printing chintzes
and not thinking about Ram?"

213

Namdev answered,
"O Trilochan, say 'Ram' with your mouth.
My hands and feet
do all the work,
but my heart is with Niranjan."

214

(by Guru Arjan Dev)

O Kabir,
I belong to no one;
no one is really mine.
I am absorbed in Him
who created all things.

215

Kabir,
the flour has fallen
into the mud.
None of it can be saved.
Only the grains
she chewed while grinding
were all that the woman really got.

216

Kabir,
the heart knows all—
but still sins.
What use is a lamp,
if you're still going to fall
into a well.

217

Kabir,
I love my Beloved.
People who don't understand
try to stop me.
How can I break off
with Him,
who has given me life
and breath?

218

Kabir,
why are you killing yourself
over houses, pavillions,
and the proper way
of decorating them?
At most, you only need half,
or a third of all this.

219

Kabir,
if I worry and fuss,
what will it accomplish?
Hari does what He likes—
my fussing won't change that.

220

(by Guru Amar Das)

He Himself creates worries,
and He Himself takes them away.
O Nanak, let us praise Him
who takes care of everything.

221

(by Guru Arjan Dev)

Kabir,
you never thought of Ram;
you were too engrossed with greed.
You died sinning:
Life vanishes in a trice.

222

Kabir,
the body is a small little pot

of unfired metal.
To keep it from breaking
you have to worship Ram—
if not, things are not going to be good.

223

Kabir,
cry out, "Keshava, Keshava";
don't sleep so carelessly.
If you cry out
day and night—
He's bound to hear you
sometime.

224

Kabir,
this body is like Kajali Forest
where elephants in heat
dwell.
Wisdom's jewel is the goad,
and one sage among many,
the mahout.

225

Kabir,
Ram is a priceless gem.
Make your mouth a wallet—
open it only before those who know
its worth.
If you come across any customers
sell it for a high price.

226

Kabir,
you never understood Ram's name;
you were busy raising a large family.
You'll die

right in the middle of everything;
you won't have time
to utter a sound.

227

Kabir,
life flits away each moment,
each time you blink.
The heart is not yet free
from snares—
and Yama comes already,
beating his kettle-drum.

228

Kabir,
Ram is a beautiful spreading tree;
its fruit is renunciation.
The sage, who has overcome all worries,
is the shade.

229

Kabir,
plant the seed
that will bear fruit
twelve months a year.
This tree's shade will be cool;
it will burgeon with fruit;
and in it birds will play.

230

Kabir,
the Giver is a tree,
mercy its fruit,
which blesses all.
When the birds fly away from it,
they say,
"O Tree, may Your fruit
be ever sweet."

231

Kabir,
you will befriend sages
if that's your fate.
You will receive the fruit of salvation
and there will be no hindrance
on the high and hazardous road.

232

Kabir,
even if for a minute,
half a minute,
a quarter of a minute,
you talk with sages—
it is all profit.

233

Kabir,
those who eat hemp,
drink wine, and eat fish—
all their baths at holy places,
fasts, and rituals
are totally wasted.

234

I lower
my eyes in shyness—
my Beloved is in my body.
I enjoy all pleasures
with my Beloved—
I tell no one.

235

For twenty-four hours,
every moment,
my soul beholds You.

Why should I
lower my eyes—
my Beloved
is in every body.

236

O faithful *sakhi*, listen,
does my body live in the Beloved,
or does the Beloved live in my body?
I cannot tell apart my body
from my Beloved.
Is my Beloved or my soul
in my body?

237

Kabir,
a Brahmin can be a guru
only for the world;
he can't be a guru for devotees:
He dies worrying
about the four Vedas.

238

Hari is sugar
scattered on sand:
An elephant cannot gather it up.
Kabir says,
"My guru gave good advice:
'Become an ant—and eat.'"

239

Kabir,
if you want to play
the game of love,
then cut off your head
and use it as a ball.
You will be so carried away

with this game
that you won't know what
is taking place.

240

Kabir,
if you want to play
the game of love,
play with a professional:
Crushing unripe mustard seeds
yields neither
oil-cakes nor oil.

241

They grope like the blind
who do not recognize sages.
Namdev says,
"How can they find Bhagwan,
without first serving His saints?"

242

Those who forsake
the diamond Hari
and yearn for some other,
will go to hell.
Ravidas speaks the truth.

243

Kabir,
if you become a householder,
then fulfill all the obligations;
if not, then renounce everything.
But if after renouncing all things,
you are still ensnared,
then you really are unlucky.

Notes

Shri Raga:

1. Normally each song contains one verse which is designated as "Rest"; it is in this verse that the "message" of the song is contained, and in singing it is used as a chorus to emphasize this message. Here there are two "Rests." The reason seems to be that the second "Rest" resolves the question raised in the first: How can a world, ensnared by Maya, understand?—by obeying the Master's command.

2. Certain sects of yogis used intoxicants to aid meditation. In view of this, Kabir speaks of ecstatic, unaided drunkenness.

Raga Gauri:

1. The "fire" is worldly longing and desire. Only the Beloved has the water to put it out. Going to the forest refers to asceticism.

4. Going around naked, shaving body hair, and retaining semen —all refer to yogic practices.

6. This song functions on the essential difference between innocence and ignorance. Religious rituals, greed, people-pleasing, lust, anger, pride amount to ignorance. Devotion leads to simple-hearted, child-like innocence.

7. In Hindu tradition, milk is ambrosial—thus it is said to run in the veins of the Brahmins. Blood, however, is considered impure, and therefore it is said to flow in the veins of the lower castes.

8. The human being is like a tree, a musical instrument, a lake. The soul is a tree's shadow, the instrument's sound, the swan upon a lake. In Indian thought, the soul is often called a swan (*hans*).

9. The opening chiasmus refers to God and his creation. Some creatures bear fruits of pearl (good deeds), while others bear fruits of glass (bad deeds).

313

12. The little well is the body; the five water-carriers are the senses.

13. The first stanza refers to the four stages of creation through which a soul moves before acquiring human shape. These are the stationary (mountains, trees, plants, etc.), the moving (animals), the crawling (insects), and the flying (winged insects, birds).

14. The last couplet is by Guru Arjan Dev, the compiler of the *Adi Granth*. It seems to provide an answer to the song's riddles or strange sights. Although the song tells us it sees through the illusion, the sport— the riddle has been solved — it does not tell us how. Guru Arjan Dev's couplet does: By thinking of the Beloved, insight is gained; and insight dispels illusion. Traditionally, this couplet is seen as part of the Kabir canon in the *Adi Granth*, as are the other additions by Guru Amar Das and Guru Arjan Dev. In view of this tradition, I have retained these instances of editorial incursion.

15. Those who die in Benares, according to Hindu tradition, instantly receive salvation. Magahar, on the other hand, is a cursed city; those that die there are reborn as donkeys. Magahar is near Gorakhpur. "To cross over" or "to swim across" is a common Indian metaphor for salvation. The world is seen as a terrible ocean; life is swimming in it; going across to the other shore is salvation.

16. Chewing *paan* (betel leaf) and flying kites are typical examples of a frivolous life in Indian tradition.

17. The "three fevers" are *adhi, viadhi, upadhi*, i.e., mental pain, bodily pain, and pain caused by external sources. The word used here for "fever" is *tap* (Sanskrit *tapas*), which literally means "bodily heat," and is related to the English "tepid," by way of the Latin *tepidus*. The primary meaning for *tapas* is physical heat resulting from ardor or fervor; its secondary meaning, "penance," "austerities" came later.

18. 'Gathering breath at the windpipe's node' refers to yogic breathing practices. The process involves breathing in through the left nostril (the *ira*), while saying "Om" (God) sixteen times. The breath is then stopped at the bridge of the nose, where the two nostrils are said to meet. I have translated this as "the windpipe's node." The breath is then slowly released through the right nostril (the *pingala*), while repeating "Om" again sixteen times.

The next step in this exercise involves forcing the breath up through the tenth door (*dasam dwar*), or the brain. When this door opens, the brain becomes heated and distills ambrosia, which then drips on to the tongue. This process is likened to the distilling process.

Turning back the Ganges and uniting it with the Jamuna refers to the Triveni (literally, "three streams"): the coming together (*sangam*) of three rivers, the Ganges, the Jamuna, and the Saraswati, at the modern city of Allahabad (known in ancient times as Prayag). The Saraswati is said to flow underground. Confluences are considered holy sites by Hindus, where pilgrims bathe. Here the implications are yogic and refer to the three breaths being turned toward the brain.

19. Through the god Brahma's agency, the Infinite, Supreme God is said to have created the world; according to Kabir, Brahma is only a courtier at God's court, as are all the other gods and goddesses — they are his creations. Brahma was the first to recite the four Vedas, which can be seen as descriptions of God. For Kabir, the Vedas, though vast, do not capture all of God's essence; thus Brahma must keep on reciting the attributes of God.

21. Literally, the last stanza reads: "Kabir says, the Bridegroom will come and unite with her — forsaking all others — who has goodness written on her forehead." Indian folk tradition says that one is born with one's destiny inscribed on one's forehead.

22. The "three worlds" (*triloka*, or *tinloka*) are heaven, earth, and the space in between. This is the traditional Hindu division. The last two lines speak of total submission to God's will, i.e., one is helpless before him. If he chooses to destroy, one must not protest.

23. The first stanza functions on an untranslateable pun. The word suttee (i.e., *sati*) literally means she who is truthful, while at the same time meaning a widow who immolates herself on her husband's pyre.

30. The 'chain of *Smriti*' is the caste system and the notion of *karma* (destiny), which binds humanity. See Glossary for *Smriti*.

32. The "five ambrosias" are milk, yogurt, butter, sugar, and honey. Traditionally, these are the best of foods.

35. Ravens as despoilers of the dead are quite an old motif, occurring in various cultures. Cf. Old Norse and Anglo-Saxon poetry where ravens, along with wolves and eagles, feast on the dead.

Raga Gauri-Guareri:

36. The four sons of Brahma are Sanaka, Sanandana, Sanatana, Sanatkumar. See Glossary.

Ragas Gauri or Sorath:

39. The "Rest" stanza likens Hari to a thug; this word comes from the Hindi *thag* meaning a "cheat" or a "swindler." Thugs were robbers who ritually strangled their victims in honor of the goddess Kali (the

practice was known as *thuggee*). Before strangulation, the victims were given a drink made from datura (the thorn-apple), which rendered them unconscious. These thugs were also known as *phansigar* ("stranglers").

41. "Impurity defiles the kitchen" refers to the upper-caste Hindu practice of daily renewing cooking utensils; used ones were considered impure. Also, each morning the cooking square and the clay-stove were daubed with fresh clay, i.e., "renewed" before use.

Raga Gauri:

42. This song is often considered to be an address to Ramananda by Kabir.

Raga Gauri-Bairagan:

45. *Sradha* is an offering of food to one's ancestors. The offering is fed to Brahmins, and also to dogs, ravens, and other birds and animals. The belief is that the food will reach the ancestors via these various agents.

47. According to yoga, there are six spheres (*cakra*) in the human body. These are: *muladhara cakra* (the sphere of the anus), *swadhishana cakra* (the sphere of the genitals), *manipura cakra* (the sphere of the navel), *anahata cakra* (the sphere of the heart), *vishudha cakra* (the sphere of the throat), and *agya cakra* (the sphere between the eyebrows). Before meditating, yogis are supposed to force breath through the *kundalini* vein, which is near the *muladhara cakra*. This is supposed to go right up to the brain (i.e., the tenth door).

Raga Gauri:

49. The "gift" is the gift of life, the gift of breath.

51. Certain yogis shave off all body hair; others just shave the head. Gosain ascetics are the followers of Gosain Datta. They tie woolen ropes

around their waists and carry begging bowls. They greet each other by saying "Alakh, Alakh" ("the invisible one"); hence they are known as *ek shabdi,* "one-worded saints."

53. Ascetics usually had both ears pierced and wore earrings; they also wore a patched cloak, and carried a pouch for ash with which they smeared their bodies, as a sign of penance. Some sects also carried deer horns that they blew; others carried *veenas* (lyres) with which they accompanied their singing.

"Triple Maya" refers to the three *gunas* or qualities (literally, "strands"), which permeate all matter: *sattva* (goodness or light), *rajas* (passion, activity), and *tamas* (darkness). These qualities are intertwined in all things. *Gunas* are also known as "virtues" or "stages" which must be overcome.

54. Here the body is compared to a full bolt of cloth; its construction resembles the process involved in weaving. The clay-pots are for water with which thread is moistened before being wound on the bobbins.

56. A cowrie is a small shell that had a very small monetary value. In idiomatic usage it means to give a thing away for free.

57. The traditional method of capturing wild bull-elephants consisted of making a wooden frame in the shape of a cow elephant, and then covering it with paper. This was placed on top of a large pit. An elephant in heat took the frame for a real cow-elephant and, in attempting to mount her, fell into the pit.

Wild monkeys were caught by filling a narrow-necked clay jar with roasted chickpeas; it was buried in the ground with the mouth exposed. A monkey would reach in and grab a handful of chickpeas; but because his clenched fist was too large for the narrow neck, he could not remove his arm, and so was captured.

Parrots were caught with a wooden barrel, hollow at both ends, propped up on two wooden sticks, above a tub full of water. Some feed placed inside the barrel attracted the parrot inside; its weight tipped the barrel over; the parrot, afraid of the water, would cling on to the inside, and thus be trapped.

The safflower (*kusumb*) was used for temporarily dyeing clothes. The petals yield a bright orange or red dye, which fades quickly in a few days.

62. It was a common Hindu belief that a child hung upside down in the womb, in a posture of penance.

65. In folk tradition, a raven is seen as a messenger. And if a raven that has been sitting on the wall of a house flies away, it means that that house can expect the return of a loved one. Ravens as harbingers also figure in Germanic tradition.

68. The widow who had decided to become a suttee was given a vermilion-filled, halved coconut. Once she took it, she could not change her mind. If she hesitated, she was forced on to the pyre.

70. Nanda was Krishna's foster-father and a cowherd in the village of Gokul; his wife's name was Yashoda. When Kamsa, the evil king of the Bhojas wanted to slay the infant Krishna, his cousin Devaki's son, Krishna's father, Vasudeva, whisked him away at night from Mathura and gave him to Nanda and Yashoda, who raised him in the village.

73. The "unique thing" is the soul. The "five watchmen" are the five senses. The "nine houses" are the nine openings of the body. The "beautiful woman" is the body itself.

The Acrostic of Kabir:

1. The Devanagari alphabet used for Sanskrit and Hindi has fifty-two letters. The Acrostic was a common device in poetry during and after Kabir's time. A verse is composed for each letter of the alphabet and the first word of each verse begins with the letter for which the verse stands. This, of course, is impossible to reproduce in translation.

5. "Turk" is a Hindu generic term for all Muslims. The "precepts" are the four methods which lead to God, according to Sufi thought. They are: *shariat* (law and ceremonies), *tarikat* (walking on the path of God), *muarfat* (divine wisdom), and *hakikat* (truth or unity with God).

19. The two "fears" here are worldly fear and the fear of God. The one induces fear, the other dispels it.

28. The fruit is divine wisdom. The "gorge" is transmigration or the cycle of birth and rebirth. Divine wisdom tears away the rind (body) and reveals the fruit within (soul).

33. The divinely illumined mind is greater than Shiva and his power (*shakti*). *Shakti* is the energetic power of a god, commonly personified as his wife.

40. The "horrid water" refers to the world's ocean of life.

Lunar Days:

Sloka. Time is seen as a river that flows without confines. In other words, time is limitless.

3. The three qualities are the three *gunas*.

6. The "six spheres" here refer not to the divisions of the body, but to the five spheres of the senses plus the sphere of the mind.

7. The "silent pool" is the *sunya* ("the void," "stillness," "silence"), which is the highest state of consciousness, where God dwells.

8. The eight elements that make up the body according to Hindu physiology are: skin, flesh, bone, marrow, fat, semen, veins, and blood.

9. The nine doors are the nine openings of the body.

12. "Twelve suns" is proverbial for enlightenment.

II. Hindus divide the moon into sixteen parts. During full moon all these are visible.

Days of the Week:

3. The "five thieves" are the senses; the "raja" is the soul.

4. Yogic thought suggests that there are two lotuses in the body: a twelve-petalled lotus in the heart, and a sixteen-petalled lotus in the brain.

5. The three gods are Brahma, Vishnu, and Shiva, themselves creations of God, and subject to good and evil.

The phrase "three rivers" primarily refers to the Triveni. By extension it can mean Maya's three *gunas* (qualities), or the meeting of the two nostrils, where the three veins (*ira, pingala, sukhmana*) come together.

Raga Asa:

1. Traditionally, this song is taken to be an address by Kabir to Ramananda. The first stanza and the rest-stanza are said to be Kabir's; the rest of the song is Ramananda's answer. "Deva" here is a polite form of address, meaning, "holy one," and does not refer to God.

2. The first stanza describes the typical garb of a Brahmin: a *dhoti* (a loin-cloth), a *janeu* (a scared thread worn by the upper twice-born castes), a *japmala* (a rosary), and a *lota* (a copper or brass jug used for bathing).

Aparas yogis do not touch metal objects.

3. "Mother" is Maya; "shirtless" means without a body; "those five" are the five senses.

4. The opening stanza alludes to tantric practices, which included eating meat, drinking wine, and having ritual sex.

The noses or ears of unfaithful wives were often cut off in Kabir's time, as a sign of infidelity. The "noseless queen" is Maya. The "five yogis" are the five senses.

5. The first line refers to "*Yogis, jatis, tapis, sanyasis,* and all those who go on *tirath.*" Yogis practice yoga; *jatis* are celibate ascetics; *tapis* are ascetics who practice *hatha yoga* ("Yoga of force," which gave the practitioner miraculous physical and psychological powers; for details, see "Yogi" in the Glossary); *sanyasis* are wandering ascetics. These represent the major forms of asceticism. *Tirath* is pilgrimage to a sacred place or shrine. There are sixty-eight such places in India.

6. The key to this riddling song is the Rest-stanza: an *akk*-pod (calotropic procera), which is bitter, becomes a sweet mango. Here metamorphosis implies improvement; thus the soul can change and improve, and become Ram.

In the morning, conchs are sounded by priests in temples to awaken the gods and summon the people to worship.

7. The "bag" is the body, which is made up of seventy-two compartments or "pockets"; the sole opening is the tenth door, or the brain.

"Nine treasures" is proverbial for all the world's wealth.

Deerskin (*mrigchhala*) was used by great and accomplished holy men as a mat to sit upon and meditate.

The four ages are the *yugas* through which creation moves. Each of these *yugas* is named after a throw of the dice: *krita* (four, cater), *treta* (trey), *dvapara* (deuce), and *kali* (ace). Their respective lengths are 4,800, 3,600, 2,400, and 1,200 "years of the gods." One year of the gods equals 360 human years. These *yugas* correspond to the four Graeco-Roman ages of gold, silver, brass, and iron. The *krita-yuga* (the golden age) was the best; our own age of iron (*kali-yuga*) is the worst. Cf. Hesiod, *The Works and Days,* 109–201.

13. This song overtly blends Hindu and Muslim concepts. The author takes his Muslim pilgrimage or *hajj,* not to Mecca, but to the river Gomti, where the Pitambar Pir (i.e., God), is found, whose song is so sweet that it enchants the heart. *Pitambar* means "yellow-robed" and is an epithet for Krishna, whose song is enchanting. *Pir* is a Muslim term for holy man. The purpose of this conjunction is stated at the end of the song: "so both Hindus and Turks may understand."

14. *Kasar* is a kind of snack made from sugar, flour, and butter.

17. Ka'aba is the sacred shrine of Islam in Mecca.

19. "She lives in a holy pool" means that Maya lives even among the holy saints.

20. The margosa is the *neem*-tree (azadirachta indica), whose fruit and leaves are extremely bitter.

21. Here the story of Ravana, the villain of the *Ramayana*, is used to expound an *ubi sunt* theme. Lanka is the island of Sri Lanka (Ceylon), which was Ravana's kingdom.

22. Some possible solutions to these riddles are as follows: the son is purity, the mother is Maya; the guru is the soul, the disciple is the heart. The lion is the soul strengthened by the name of Ram (see the last couplet); the cattle are the subdued senses. A water-dwelling fish is the soul dwelling within the company of saints, who are like water; a soul's existence is as unreal as a fish laying eggs on a tree (the world). The cat is lust, the dog patience. The tree (world) has spread its branches to the earth for support and shot up its roots (meditation upon God). The flowers and fruits are lust and greed. The buffalo is desire, the horse is the heart; the ox is patience, and the load it was carrying has fallen on the soul.

23. The pit of fire is the womb.

24. The soul is the bride and God the bridegroom. Cf. Christ as bridegroom.

The five virtues are *karaj* (work, action), *sat* (truth), *santokh* (patience, contentment), *daya* (mercy), and *dharma* (righteousness, religion).

Walking around the fire refers to the Hindu marriage ceremony, where the couple circumambulates the sacred fire seven times.

Literally, "In the lotus of my breath" reads, "in the lotus of my navel." The navel is the gathering point of breath.

A Hindu marriage is performed under a wooden canopy or pavilion (*vedi*). The canopy is supported by four wooden poles; under it two reed baskets are placed upside down, upon which the couple sits. "Marriage mantras" (charms or spells) are verses from the Vedas, invoking well-being and fertility, which are intoned during the ceremony.

25. This song describes the anguish of a new bride trying to cope with her in-laws. Since marriages were arranged and families lived jointly in Kabir's time, a newly married woman had to contend with all of her husband's family. Folk tradition is full of songs, proverbs, and anecdotes describing the enmity between a new wife and her mother-in-law. Traditionally, the husband's youngest brother is sympathetic towards the bride. On a metaphysical level, the bride is the soul; the mother-in-law is Maya; the father-in-law is worldly love; the eldest brother-in-law is death (Yama); the five senses are the sisters-in-law; the husband is God; the wife's eldest brother is wisdom.

In folk songs, a wife often complains to her brother who has come to see her for the first time in her new home. This song participates in this "complaint" tradition.

26. It is said that this song was a reply to a Brahmin who told Kabir that because of his low caste he had no business dabbling in religion.

Brahmins are commonly called *gosain,* or cowherds, who look after other people (cows).

28. The first stanza speaks of the 840,000 lives that a soul moves through before attaining human birth. The lute is worldly love or attachment.

31. "Guru" here refers to a human teacher and does not mean God. The swan (*hans*), according to Hindu tradition, eats pearls, because it alone can discern them; the crane, on the other hand, sees only the waves. The swan can also separate milk from water with its beak.

32. This song is often read very literally, and has led to the belief that Kabir had two wives, the first ugly, the second beautiful. But we must recognize allegory: The soul (the bride) without God is ugly; the soul in love with God is beautiful.

33. The first stanza can also be translated as follows:

At first my daughter-in-law was called Dhanya;
now they call her Ramjanya.

The key word in this contention is *bahuria;* it derives from the Sanskrit *vadhu, vadhuti,* meaning both "a bride," "a young wife," "a young woman," or a "daughter-in-law." Traditionally, the first and the Rest stanzas are considered to be complaints made by Kabir's mother. First of all, she is angry that the "baldheads" (ascetics) are calling her daughter-in-law Ramjanya, whose real name is Dhanya. Her anger stems from the fact that Ramjanya in the parlance of the day meant temple prostitute (literally, "God's or Ram's handmaid"). Secondly, she complains that Kabir is neglecting his work and busying himself with asceticism.

The problem with such an explanation is that it forces the assumption that Kabir had two wives; we know that Kabir's wife's name was Loi. But again the song is allegorical: If Ramjanya means "Ram's handmaid," then Dhanya should also mean something. And it does; literally, "wealthy," or "one who loves or acquires wealth." The ugly first wife, Dhanya, is Maya, who loved worldly pleasures and wealth. The beautiful second wife loves Ram. It is the saints who have made the divorce and second marriage possible; they destroyed the first house and built a second, where the heart, the little son, can say "Ram" without fear.

34. The traditional explanation for this song states that it is Kabir's admonition to his daughter-in-law against the custom of veiling. Again, an allegorical explanation leads to a better understanding of the text: The soul, the new bride, veils her face from her husband Ram; the previous wife, the previous state of the soul, never removed her veil, and thus never saw her Beloved.

35. The narrative traditionally constructed around this song stems from a mistranslation. The last stanza reads in the original:

> Kahat Kabir, sunoh re loi,
> Ab tumri partiti na hoi.

Kahat (says), Kabir, *sunoh* (listen), *re* (O), *loi* (world), *ab* (now), *tumri* (on you), *partiti* (trust, faith), *na* (not, no longer), *hoi* (will have, can have).

As mentioned earlier, Kabir's wife was called Loi; and since *re loi* appears here, it has naturally been assumed that Kabir is angry with his wife and will never again trust her. The story goes that once Loi refused to cook for an ascetic who had come to visit Kabir. This led to a quarrel. The first four stanzas are therefore considered to be Loi's attempts at making up; the last stanza is considered to be Kabir's peevish reply. But a closer reading makes this narrative unnecessary.

Loi is preceded by *re*, which is a masculine interjection; its feminine version would be *ri*. Thus if Kabir was talking to his wife, he would say, *"ri Loi"* (O Loi), and not *re Loi*. Thus *loi* here means the world, and is not a name. The song is a petition to God, asking him not to turn his back, for Kabir now no longer trusts the world.

37. Haramba is another name for Magahar, where death leads to rebirth as a donkey.

Raga Sorath:

1. *Kapris* are a sect of ascetics who cover themselves completely with cloaks.

Kedar is a shrine in the Himalayas, sacred to Shiva.

2. "Hung upside down" refers to the foetus, which was thought to stay in the womb for ten months.

3. *Nadis* are yogis who play a kind of horn; *bedis* are the readers of the Vedas, or the ritualists; *shabdis* are ascetics who follow the teachings of Gosain Datta; *munis* are ascetics who never speak.

4. Creation is God's drama, in which he is the main actor. He ends the play in his own time, for his own pleasure.

5. The "poor girl" (the soul) wanders from house to house (transmigrates); she is collared by worldly love and fettered by groundless hopes and wishes.

6. "A son begets the father": the soul gives birth to God the father, i.e., the soul places Him inside itself. "A city is built/ where there

was no room": that which seemed useless becomes essential. Cf. Christ's parable of the cornerstone.

10. The "wild animals" are lusts. The "lotus-pitcher" is the heart. The "water" is wickedness and sin. It is said that the hearts of ordinary people are upended; those of saints stand right side up.

Raga Dhanashri:

4. "Indra's city or Shiva's city" are epithets for heaven.

5. Ajamala the Brahmin fell in love with a prostitute and lived with her all his life, enjoying worldly pleasures. One of his sons was named Narayana (an epithet for Vishnu). When Ajamala was near death, he called out to his son, and because he had spoken God's name as well, he achieved salvation.

"The elephant" was really a celestial musician who had been cursed and given the form of an elephant. One day as he went to a lake to drink, an octopus seized him. Unable to free himself, the elephant prayed to God and lifted up a water-lily as an offering. This act saved him from the octopus and freed him from the curse.

"The prostitute" was given a parrot by an ascetic who wanted to save her from a life of sin. This parrot knew how to say "Ram." Hearing it continually say God's name, the prostitute also took up the refrain—and was saved.

These anecdotes are all from the Puranas.

Raga Tilang:

1. "The Western holy books" refers primarily to Islam.

Raga Suhi:

2. "Bumblebees leave; cranes now alight and sit" refers to hair once dark turning grey.

Raga Suhi-Lalit:

5. The "fort" is the body, the "lords" are the five senses. Death is the "accountant." The body's nine openings are the "surveyors"; the five organs of perception and the five organs of action are the "ten judges." The "seventy-two houses" are the sections that make up the human body.

Raga Bilawal:

7. The four blessings are *dharma* (faith), *artha* (wealth), *kama* (fulfillment of desires), and *moksha* (salvation).

11. The phrase "the three breaths" refers to yogic distinctions: the breaths in the two nostrils and in the bridge of the nose. Here, these "breaths" can also be the tripartite structuring of divine wisdom or knowledge: *gyata* (the Knower, i.e., God), *gyan* (knowledge), and *geya* (the content of knowledge).

Raga Gaund:

3. "The four realms" are the four cardinal points: north, south, east, west.

4. This song describes a failed attempt by Muslims to kill Kabir.

"The fourth stage" (*chautha pada*) is the achievement of salvation. It can be achieved when one overcomes the three *gunas,* i.e., matter itself. Perhaps this is why it is called the fourth stage; because one has to move through each of the three *gunas,* in order to overcome them, and achieve salvation, the fourth quality, virtue, stage.

5. The "he" in this song is the soul, which is considered to be God's reflection.

Udasis are a sect of mendicants; sheikhs are Muslim religious leaders.

7. The "wife" here is Maya.

8. The "five Naradas" are the five senses. They can also be the five evils: lust, pride, anger, greed, and worldly love. Narada was one of Brahma's mind-born sons. See Glossary.

Raga Ramkali:

1. According to Hindu myth, there are fourteen worlds, seven above the Earth and seven below, including the earth.

2. Flowers of the *mahua*-tree (bassia latifolia) were used in the fermentation process.

5. On the fourteenth and fifteenth of the month, Brahmins performed various ceremonies for good fortune.

6. The "tree" is the world; the "shoots" and "branches" are the various living things. The "bumblebee" is the God-intoxicated soul. The "beautiful plant" is solace that sucks up the "waters" of worldly desires.

7. Yogis smeared their bodies with ash as a sign of their renunciation of the world.

The five virtues are patience, truth, work, mercy, and righteousness.

10. The "binder" is Maya. The "snake's circle" is the *kundalini* vein, which leads to the tenth door (the brain). Metaphorically, "the moon has swallowed the sun" can be patience (considered cool like moonlight) overcoming hot desires.

Raga Maru:

2. Antimony was used as eye make-up and was thought to prevent eye diseases such as glaucoma.

9. This song is Krishna's reply to Duryodhana, who complained that when Krishna was in Hastinapur he chose to spend the night with a poor man named Vidura, rather than in Duryodhana's vast palace. This story occurs in the *Mahabharata*.

Slokas I & II. In the *Adi Granth*, these two Slokas are placed after hymn 9. I am following this order and leaving them here rather than incorporating them with the main body of Slokas.

Raga Kedara:

1. For the "three virtues," see *Gauri* 53. The "fourth virtue" is the same as the fourth stage (*Gaund* 4).

Raga Bhairo:

4. Devout Muslims pray five times a day.

10. "Shiva's city" is the brain, the tenth door, which leads to perception and understanding of the Beloved. Once this realization is achieved, self-pride vanishes. At this stage the moon's watery light (patience) extinguishes the sun's (lust's) raging fire. The sun now rises in the east and in the west, i.e., there is no room for darkness; everything is engulfed in light (enlightenment). The "western door," where the sun sets, is the place of darkness and ignorance; the threshold allows one to ascend to the window, the tenth door, where limitless, boundless illumination awaits.

11. "Rama" refers to Rama Chandra, the incarnation of Vishnu, and the hero of the epic the *Ramayana*. He is not the same as "Ram," the unfathomable, unincarnated God of Kabir's verse. In order to differentiate between the two, I have chosen to place the final "a," usually present in anglicizations of Sanskrit, in the former's name.

13. A *jati* is a celibate ascetic; six *jatis* is proverbial for the entire sect. The "nine *Naths*" are the masters of great yogic and magical powers, believed to have been nine in number. The *Siddhas* are also wonder workers who acquired great prowess through extreme penance and yoga; traditionally, they are eighty-four of them. The "five angels," here, refers to the five senses.

15. The various numbers in this song have no particular significance; they signify God's vastness and power.

16. The fortress is the body.

17. The "two walls" refer to the dualism of soul and matter. The "three moats" are the three qualities (*gunas*). The "five" are the senses; the "twenty-five" are the categories of Sankhya philosophy, one of the oldest schools of Indian philosophic thought.

Sankhya is one of the "Six Doctrines" in the classification of philosophy commonly known as *Shaddarsana*, which consists of Nyaya, Vaisheshika, Sankhya, Yoga, Mimamsa, and Vedanta.

The Sankhya system was founded by the sage Kapila. It proposed a dualistic approach (the static *purusha*—the soul—and the active *prakrti*—matter), and atheism. Its twenty-five categories (*tattva*) are:

(1) *Prakrti* ("matter"), which leads to creation and initiates evolution, not through the agency of a god, but because that is its nature. It leads to (2) *buddhi* (insight, intelligence), which brings about (3) *ahankara* (self-consciousness).

From *ahankara* arise the five invisible elements (*tanmatras*), namely, (4) ether (*akasa*), (5) air, (6) light, (7) water, (8) earth. These elements produce the five visible or material elements (*mahabhutas*) which are part of everyday reality: (9) fire, (10) air, (11) earth, (12) water, and (13) sky.

Ahankara gives rise to the five organs of the senses (*jnanindriyas*): (14) smell, (15) touch, (16) taste, (17) hearing, and (18) vision, and the five organs of action (*karmindriyas*): (19) speech, (20) holding, (21) walking, (22) excretion, and (23) reproduction.

The last category produced by *ahankara* is (24) *manas* (the mind), which harmonizes the external world with the internal organs. The twenty-fifth *tattva* is completely separate, and lies outside the realm of *prakrti,* and is (25) the *purusha* (the soul, literally, "the being"). The *purusha,* inert and static, merely watches the evolution of *prakrti;* neither is dependent upon the other. The soul achieves salvation by realizing that it is different from *prakrti.*

Sankhya thought introduced the concept of the three *gunas* or qualities (*sattva, rajas,* and *tamas*) already discussed. *Prakrti* contains these three elements or virtues in equal proportion. But as evolution progresses, these elements become distributed in varying proportions. Sankhya was later modified, and *purusha* came to be regarded as an active creator (god), and *prakrti* came to be seen as "his" goddess wife.

20. Clouds are traditionally seen as messengers, as in Kalidasa's *Meghaduta* ("Cloud-Messenger"). "Horrid black goddesses" are Kali the bloody aspect of the goddess Devi. "Those who defeated Ravana's army" refers to Rama Chandra, the hero of the epic *Ramayana.* "Those in the Puranas" refers to Krishna, whose deeds are described in *The Bhagavata Purana.*

Raga Basant:

2. Kalyuga is the present era, the most degenerate, which will end in destruction. Vishnu will appear at the end of the Kalyuga epoch, the present one, riding a white horse and holding a flaming sword. He will

destroy evil and the wicked; he will reward the good; and he will restore the first Golden Age.

3. This song describes the perversions that prevail in the present age (Kalyuga), which include confusion of castes, disintegration of morality, the abandonment of religion, and the rule of cruel kings.

4. The god Vishnu took on an incarnation (*avatara*) whenever moral order began to decay in the world, taking on ten incarnations in all. This song refers to the fourth incarnation in order to elaborate the point that God protects his worshippers. Vishnu became a fish (Matsya), a tortoise (Kurma), a boar (Varaha), a man-lion (Narsinha), a dwarf (Vamana), Rama with the Axe (Parashurama), Rama of Ayodhya—the hero of the *Ramayana*, Krishna, the Buddha, and he will become Kalka, which has not yet taken place.

5. Madana ("the maddener"), or Kama, the god of love, has stolen the gem of divine wisdom, i.e., lust has driven out wisdom.

When Vishnu, the all-pervader, slept in the primordial ocean of the cosmos, a lotus sprouted from his navel, and from that lotus emerged Brahma, who created the world. When the creation process was completed, Vishnu awoke and began to rule the world.

6. The "one merchant" is the body, the "five shopkeepers," the senses. The "twenty-five oxen" are the categories of Sankhya philosophy. The "nine staffs" are the nine openings of the body, while the "ten sacks" are the ten breaths in the body, as enumerated by the yogis. According to yogic physiology, there are seventy-two arteries and veins, "the ropes," that keep the body functioning.

The "seven threads" can be the five senses plus understanding and the mind; or they can be *vairaga* (abandoning worldliness), *viveka* (discernment), *khata sampata* (the six acquisitions), *moksha* (hope of deliverance), *srawana* (hearing about God), *manana* (obeying God), and *nididhyasana* (unswerving meditation). (The "six acquisitions" are *sama* [controlling the mind], *dama* [controlling the senses], *uprati* [neither hating or loving], *tatiksha* [bearing pain], *shradha* [faith], and *samadhanta* [heeding a guru's advice].) The "seven threads" can also be construed as lust, pride, worldly love, greed, anger, vain hope, and desire. More simply, the phrase can be idiomatic for many kinds of ordinary thread.

The "three tax-collectors" are the *gunas;* the "trader" is the soul; the "caravan" is the body.

Raga Basant-Hindola:

7. Here the Hindu notions of religious purity and impurity are being repudiated. "The cooking square" is where the actual cooking is done. Orthodox Hindus ritually cleanse it each time the area is used.

Raga Basant:

8. There is a traditional story connected with this song: Once a stray dog stole into Kabir's house, ate what it could find, and spoiled the rest. Seeing this, Kabir sang this song. On the allegorical level, it becomes a comment on the human life-span: A person is born, looks about, eats, and dies. There is the constant danger of being hit by a stick or a brick, i.e., death looms ever near. Cf. Bede's exemplum of a sparrow flying into a bright hall from the darkness, lingering for a while, and then flying away again.

Raga Parbhati:

2. The Jagannath festival is a famous pilgrimage site in Puri, where Vishnu is worshipped as "Lord of the world" (*jagannath*). *Pir* is a Muslim religious guide.

4. *"Halal"* is food ritually purified in the Muslim context, i.e., making food, especially meat, holy and fit to be eaten.

5. "All kinds of instruments" literally reads: "The five kinds of instruments," namely, the human voice, stringed instruments, instruments made from animal skins (drums), those made from metal (cymbals), and wind instruments.

Slokas of Kabir:

All the Slokas begin with an address to Kabir. This is a convention frequently found in the *Adi Granth*. There is some rigidity about this because some slokas also have the signature (*bhanita*) at the end. See for example, nos. 36, 54, 55, 62, 69, 82, 84, 117, 141, 171, 182. The majority of the Slokas, however, only have the name "Kabir" in the beginning.

8. "She," here, is pride or worldly love; once she is repulsed, she bows in obeisance and leaves.

9. "Her" is Maya or pride.

11. "Forest trees" in the original reads "*palas*-trees" which are the butea frondosa. They are not used for anything; their bright red flowers have no fragrance.

19. Iced water was poured into the churn to help congeal the butter and facilitate its separation from the whey.

31. Kabir is playing with the literal meaning of his name, which means "great," and as an appellation for God.

42. The "house" is the body; the "five sons" are the passions: pride, greed, lust, anger, worldly love.

43. The "son" or "daughter" are the senses. Further, the "son" can be the soul and the body, the "daughter."

47. The "foreigner's coat" is the body that travels through life. The "fire" is death, which consumes this coat completely; the "thread" is the soul, which holds the coat together but remains unscathed by the fire, i.e., the soul is immortal.

49. The "fish" is humankind; the "pond" is Maya in whose nets people are entangled and caught. But if the fish swims out to the "wide sea" (God's protection), it will be safe.

53. The "lean stag" is the soul, weary of the long chase of birth and rebirth; the "lake" is the world. The "hunters" are wicked deeds, ever ready to pounce upon the soul.

56. Turmeric and lime were mixed together to form a red mixture used as a ceremonial dye in religious rituals. In order to make this mixture, both ingredients have to lose their distinguishing properties—such is the union of God and the individual soul.

65. Henna was put on the soles of the feet in summertime, since it was believed to have cooling properties.

74. "Motia" (pearl) is a typical name for dogs, like "Rover" or "Fido."

78. Holding on to someone's sleeve signifies seeking that person's protection.

83. See note to Sloka 42, above.

91. This is a difficult Sloka to unravel. There is a traditional story used to explain it: One day, by the banks of the Ganges, Kabir saw a hunter shoot a deer, a doe with two calves in her womb. Thus with the death of the mother, both the calves died. The buck came a little later and was also killed by the hunter's arrow. When the hunter went to undo the animals, he was bitten by a snake and died. When his wife heard about this, she came running to the spot where her husband lay, and upon seeing him died of grief. Thus all told, six beings died: four males and two females.

On the allegorical level, we can find the following meaning: when one kills the heart (by depriving it of lusts and desires), pride and worldly love die. When these two die, desire and love of the body die. With the death of these four, evil and malice die off, bringing the total to six. Of these, the first four grammatically are masculine in gender, while the last two are feminine.

103. The "instrument" is the body; the "player" is life.

107. A childless Hindu woman would go to the cremation ground where a body had been recently burned and say appropriate spells and mantras. Then she would return to her home, strip naked, cook bread, and eat it. The desired results were two-fold: to cause the death of the children in the family of the person recently cremated, and to induce fertility in the barren woman. This ritual was called *masan jagana* ("to awaken or reanimate the dead in the cremation ground").

108. Hoi is the goddess of smallpox. In the month of October, her image would be painted on walls, or clay statues would be made in her honor. Women would fast during this period in order to gain the goddess's favour. Most Hindu gods and goddesses have various mounts that they ride: She rides a donkey. She is also known as Sanjhi ("the friend").

109. "Stilts" refers to the tricks of dancers and jugglers, who perform daring feats.

115. Tradition states that Kabir had two children: a son named Kamal and a daughter named Kamali, meaning "intelligent." In this regard, this Sloka has also been rendered as follows:

Kabir's family drowned
when this son Kamal
was born.
Forgetting Hari
he brought home wealth.

The story explaining this version says that once Kamal met a leper by the banks of the Ganges who was going to drown himself. Kamal got him to desist with the promise that he could get him cured. He took some Ganges water in his palm, blew upon it, and sprinkled it on the leper. The leper was instantly healed. In gratitude, he richly rewarded Kamal. When Kamal brought home what he had been given, Kabir spoke this Sloka as a remonstrance to his son for falling prey to the lure of wealth.

On the allegorical level, we find that in many of these songs, "son" is used as an epithet for the heart. "Kamal" means intelligent; but it can also be used in an ironic or even sarcastic manner. And that seems to be the sense at work here. Thus Kabir's family would drown (in the ocean of the world) if his heart forsook God, and, thinking itself very cunning or brilliant, would be deluded by wealth or worldly love.

119. The "You" here does not properly refer to "Kabir." The name "Kabir" in the beginning is an identity tag. However, on the level of discourse, we can say that "Kabir" ("Great"), a Muslim epithet for God, is the addressee of this Sloka.

124. The chatrik is the Indian pied cuckoo. Tradition states that it lives only on those raindrops that fall when the moon is full. Its cries are considered plaintive and have the power to burst love's unhealed wounds. It is also called *sarang* and *papihu*.

125. The chakava is the ruddy sheldrake or the brahmani duck. These ducks live in pairs and are said to be the souls of pining lovers. With the setting sun, they must part; and all night long they call out to each other and await the dawn when they can be reunited.

126. In temples, priests sound the conch-shell at dawn to awaken the gods and summon worshippers.

137. "Paper prisons" are holy books that seal off the heart from truly experiencing divinity; the "stones" are idols.

152. "Where the Ganges and the Jamuna meet" could mean the yogic distinction between the breath of the left and the right nostrils and the point of their meeting; or that the place of purity, the place of unmoving silence, where God resides, should be chosen as one's abode.

158. A flute (the soul) is useless without a flautist (the True Guru); someone has to blow the music inherent in it.

161. The "truss" is divine wisdom, or the guru's word.

175. Malaya mountain was noted for its sandal trees in Kabir's time.

187. This *sloka* is an admonition to Muslims who sacrifice animals to God.

190. The *Ras-Leela* is a dramatic depiction of Krishna's amorous adventures with the women of Gokul, the village of his youth.

191. The "One" Ram is the all-pervasive God; the "other" Ram is Rama Chandra, who pervaded his own body only. Kabir is here differentiating between his own use of the name Ram, and the common, popular understanding of Ram (i.e., Rama the hero of *The Ramayana*, one of Vishnu's incarnations).

198. "Pir" (a Muslim religious adept) in this Sloka refers to God.

202. The duality is that between matter and soul, as outlined in Sankhya philosophy. The "six types of ascetics" are *yogis* (who practise yoga), *jangamas* (who mat their hair and put chains on their feet), *sarevras* (who shave their heads), *sanyasis* (who have abandoned the world), *boddhis* (Buddhist monks), and *vairagis* (worshippers of Vishnu who wear sacrificial threads).

212. Namdev and Trilochan are two famous 13th-century *bhakti*-poets.

233. "Hemp" is the narcotic *bhang (cannabis indica)*, which is frequently taken by ascetics as a meditational aid. Eating fish and drinking refer to the Tantric ritual of defilement, where things forbidden were done in order to rise towards the state of bliss.

235. There are no *slokas* by Namdev or Ravidas in the *Adi Granth*. Traditionally, this and number 241 are considered as Kabir's own compositions.

Glossary

Ajamala a Brahmin of Kanauj who lived a very worldly life and married a prostitute. One of his sons he named Narayana, which is an epithet for Vishnu. On his death bed, he called out to his son and obtained salvation because he finally uttered God's name.

Akrura the uncle of Krishna. He was sent by Kamsa, the evil king of the Bhojas, to bring Krishna from Gokul so he could be slain. Akrura went to do this against his will. When he arrived in Gokul, Krishna saw his unwillingness and revealed to him his own divine nature.

Antarjami ("knower of the innards," "knower of hidden desires") an epithet for the attributeless God.

atma the soul, life-breath. Cf. German *der Atem*.

Bedi a reader of the Vedas.

bairagi
(vairagi) an ascetic or mendicant who has renounced all worldly desires and pleasures and who feels neither passion nor desire.

Banwari ("lord of the forest") an epithet for Krishna.

Beethal
(Vitthal) an epithet for Krishna as he is worshipped in southern India. The name derives from the Sanskrit *vishthal* ("he who is far away").

Benares (Varanasi)	a holy city on the eastern Ganges. Since it is Shiva's city, the common belief is that those who die there obtain immediate salvation.
Bhakti	Hindu religious system of mystical love for a personalized God.
Bhagwan	("dispenser of treasure") an epithet for Krishna.
Bhupati	("lord of the earth") an appellation for God.
Bindraban	("forest of basil") the forest where Krishna played during his childhood and youth, sporting and frolicking with the milkmaids.
Brahma	("the creator") the first member of the Hindu trinity, who created the world, the universe, and the Vedas. He has four heads and four arms. His wife is Saraswati, the goddess of learning and the arts. His vehicle is the swan.
Brahmin	the highest, priestly caste. Brahmins are said to be the first among all created things. The major function of a Brahmin is to memorize, study, and pass on the Vedas, and to perform religious rituals, sacrifices, and ceremonies.
Chaturbhuj	("the four-armed") an epithet for the god Vishnu.
Chhatrapati	("lord of the umbrella") an epithet for God, whose umbrella is the sky. The umbrella was emblematic of a ruler in India.
Chitragupta	("visible invisible") the recording scribe of Yama, god of the dead, keeping accounts of the good and bad deeds of human beings.
Damodar	("roped around the belly") a designation for Krishna. In his childhood, his foster-mother, Yashoda, tied him up with a rope as punishment for various pranks.

Dayal   ("merciful") a name for God.

Deva   ("far-shining") God or deity. Cf. Latin *deus, divus,*
                 and Greek *theos.*

Devi   ("far-shining") feminine form of God. Cf. Latin
                 dea, Greek *thea.*

Dharmraja   ("king of justice") a name for Yama, the lord of the
                 Hindu underworld.

Dharnidhar   ("keeper of the earth") God.

Dhruva   ("fixed," "constant") a sage of antiquity. As a child
                 he was disinherited from his rightful throne by his
                 cousin. He became an ascetic and put himself
                 through a rigorous discipline. His austerities
                 gained him the favor of Vishnu, who transformed
                 him into the pole-star, which remains forever
                 fixed.

Dinanatha   ("lord of the poor") namely, God.

Dindayal   ("merciful to the poor") God.

Duryodhana   ("hard to defeat") one of the villains in the epic, the
                 Mahabharata, who refused to give up the kingdom
                 of the Kurus to its rightful rulers, the five Panda-
                 vas, one of whom was Arjuna, to whom Krishna re-
                 vealed his divine nature and recited the *Bhagawad
                 Gita.* In the battle between the Kurus and the Pan-
                 davas, Duryodhana was killed, and the Pandavas
                 recovered their kingdom.

Ganesha   ("lord of hosts") the elephant-headed son of Shiva.
                 He is the god of wisdom and the remover of hard-
                 ships.

Garuda   ("devourer") the bird on which Vishnu rides. He is
                 represented as having the head, beak, wings, and
                 talons of an eagle, and the body of a man.

gayatri	("song") the most sacred verse of the *Rig Veda*, recited every morning and evening by Hindus. The text runs: "Let us meditate upon the beautiful radiance of the god Savitr that he may illumine our minds." Savitr ("animator") is the sun-god.
Gobind (Govind)	("lord of cowherds," "binder of cows," "keeper of cows") an epithet for Krishna.
Gomti	a river in Oude, in eastern India.
Gopal	("keeper of cows") an epithet for Krishna.
Gosain (Goswami)	("master of cows") an appellation for God; also used as a form of address for Brahmins.
Guna	the three qualities which permeate all matter in varying degrees: *sattva* (light, goodness), *rajas* (action, passion), *tamas* (dullness, darkness, sluggishness). They are also virtues, stages, and levels of being.
guru	("authority") a teacher or guide who shows the path to truth. The word is also used as a title for God, who is called the "True Guru."
hajj	pilgrimage that Muslims make to the Ka'aba in Mecca.
halal	Muslim dietary principles, similar to the Jewish concept of "kosher"; it especially refers to properly bled meat.
hans	("swan") an appellation for the soul in Indian thought.
Hanuman	("large jaws") the monkey king in the *Ramayana* who helped Rama rescue his wife, Sita, from the evil king, Ravana. As a reward for this service, Rama gave Hanuman eternal life and youth.

Haramba (Magahar)	the village where Kabir is traditionally said to have died.
Hari	("lord," "resplendent") a title for Vishnu.
Harnakhasa	("golden-eyed") a devotee of Shiva and father of Prahlada.
Hoi	the goddess of smallpox.
Indra	("leader," "the first") king of the gods, who wields the thunderbolt and sends the rain. Cf. Jove, Jupiter.
Jagannath	(master of the world) God; also an epithet for Vishnu.
Jagdish	("lord of the world") namely, God.
Jagjivan	("life of the world") God.
Jaidev (Jayadeva)	famous Sanskrit poet of the eleventh century A.D., who composed the *Gitu Govinda,* "Govind's (i.e., Krishna's) Song," an erotic poem which describes Krishna's youthful love for Radha.
jati	a celibate ascetic.
Ka'aba	the square building within the Great Mosque in Mecca, where Muslims go on pilgrimage, the *hajj.*
Kailash	a mountain in the Himalayas near Lake Manas. Shiva's paradise is located here.
Kajuli Forest	near Hardwar, in northwestern India, famous for its elephants.
Kali	("black") the terrible and bloody aspect of the goddess *Durga* ("impassable"), the great goddess (Devi) and wife of Shiva. As the female energy

(*shakti*) of the god, she assumes two forms: one gentle, the other fierce. It is this fierce aspect that is often worshipped when she is called "the black, fierce, terrible one," i.e., Kali, who has ten arms, with a weapon in each hand. As Durga, she is portrayed as a beautiful woman, riding a tiger with a grim expression on her face.

Kalkin
(Kalka) — ("strife," "impure") the tenth incarnation of Vishnu, which has yet to appear. In apocalyptic fashion, Vishnu will appear mounted on a white horse, with a blazing, comet-like sword and will destroy evil forever, restore purity, and rejuvenate creation.

Kalyuga — the present era, the age of iron, which is more degraded than all the previous ages. In all, there are four ages according to the Hindu scheme of things, each one more degenerate than the last.

Kama — ("desire") the god of love, who smites humans with his arrows of love. Cf. Eros and Cupid.

Kamla — ("lotus") another name for the goddess of beauty and fortune (see Lakshmi).

Kamlakant — ("Kamla's husband") Vishnu

Kamlapati — ("Kamla's lord") Vishnu.

kapri — ("clothed") an ascetic who covers his entire body, including the face, with cloth.

Karim — ("merciful") a Muslim designation for God.

Kedara
(Kedarnatha) — a Hindu place of pilgrimage in the Himalayas, sacred to Shiva.

Keshava — ("long-haired") an epithet for Vishnu.

Khimakar   ("forgiver") God.

Khuda   Persian, hence Muslim, name for God.

Kirpal   ("merciful") God.

Kratar   ("creator") God.

Krishna   ("dark") the eighth and most popular incarnation
                  of Vishnu. Krishna and his older brother were
                  raised by foster-parents in a little village because
                  their maternal cousin, Kamsa, wanted to kill them;
                  it had been foretold that his aunt's eighth son
                  (Krishna) would kill Kamsa. As a youth, Krishna
                  enchanted the women of the village, and his favor-
                  ite among them was Radha. When Krishna grew
                  up, he slew Kamsa, and took the throne. However,
                  he was forced out by Kamsa's father-in-law. After
                  his flight, he went on to found the city of Dwarika.
                  In the *Mahabharata* he aided the Pandavas in their
                  fight against the Kauravas (Kurus); and it is as the
                  charioteer of Arjuna that he reveals himself as
                  Vishnu and recites the *Bhagavad Gita*. He is said to
                  have died (Achilles-like) when a hunter, mistaking
                  him for a deer in the thicket, shot an arrow into his
                  heel — his only vulnerable spot.

Kubera   ("ugly-shaped") a semi-divine lord of wealth, and
(Kuvera)   guardian of the Himalayas. He is the king of the
                  Yakshas, semi-divine spirits who are generally be-
                  nevolent but also have malevolent tendencies.

Lakshmi   ("lucky," "good-fortuned") wife of Vishnu, god-
                  dess of fortune and beauty. She sprang from the
                  ocean's froth, glowing with beauty, when the gods
                  churned the waters. Cf. the birth of Aphrodite.

Lanka   the island kingdom of Ravana, who abducted Sita,
                  wife of Rama Chandra.

Madana   ("inflamer") an appellative for the god of love (see Kama).

Madho   ("spring-like") Krishna's family name; thus liter-
(Madhava)   ally it means "descended from Madhu." Madhu was an ancestor of Krishna.

Madhusudan   ("slayer of Madhu") Krishna, who slew the demon Madhu, which is not the same name as Krishna's family.

Magahar   a city in northeastern India. Legend has it that those who die here are reborn as donkeys. It is also known as Haramba.

Mahadeva   ("great god") one of Shiva's names.

Mahesha   ("great lord") Shiva.
(Mahesh-
wara)

Mahua   the bassia latifolia whose flowers were used in fermenting liquor.

Mansarowar   a holy lake in the Himalayas. In Kabir's verse it symbolizes *sunya,* the infinite silence, which is the soul's resting place.

Marka   a semi-divine descendent of Brahma.

Maya   ("magical illusion") the unreality of all creation. It is often personified as a goddess.

Meru   ("golden mountain") a mythic mountain said to be
(Sumeru)   the center of the earth. On its peak is located Indra's heaven, and it is the dwelling place of all the gods and other celestial beings. Cf. Mount Olympus, Asgard.

Mukanda   ("giver of salvation") God.

Mullah	a Muslim spiritual leader.
Muni	("silent") a holy seer and ascetic who through severe austerities has obtained semi-divine status.
Murari	("slayer of Mura") an epithet for Krishna, who slew the demon Mura and his seven thousand sons. A vow of silence was one of their characteristics.
Nadi	Yogis who characteristically play a kind of a horn (*nad*).
Namdev	a thirteenth century *bhakti*-poet who lived in the Bombay area. He was a tailor by caste; many of his songs survive.
Nanda	("bliss") Krishna's foster-father and head of the village of Gokul where Krishna was raised, to escape the wrath of Kamsa, the evil king.
Narada	a son of Brahma and a sage, who demanded from the unattributeless God the secret of Maya. In order to teach him, Vishnu appeared to him and advised him that he would have to carry out various exploits, thereby learning about Maya. One of these involved his being turned into a woman: Cf. Teiresias. Narada also had a reputation for being very ill-tempered. When Brahma advised him to marry, he accused his father of leading him astray from his devotions. Angered, Brahma cursed him to a life of promiscuity; Narada, in turn, cursed his father as committing incest and as a god not worthy of adoration.
Narayana	("man's son," "born of water") an appellation for Vishnu.
Narsinha (Narsingha)	("man-lion") Vishnu's fourth incarnation when he slew the father of his devotee, Prahlada (see Harnakhasa).

Naunayak   ("lord of the nine") God. The "nine" refer to the nine regions that constitute the entirety of the earth.

Niranjan   ("without fault," "unstained") God.

Nirankar   ("without form") God.

Nirgun   ("without attributes") the supreme being (God), who is unqualifiable, absolute, and beyond form. All the gods, celestial beings, the world, and the universe are his creation.

Parbrahma   ("beyond Brahma") the supreme God, whom all other gods serve.

Parmeshwar   ("the highest lord") God.

Parvidgar   ("keeper," perhaps a contracted form of the Persian Parvardigar) God the cherisher.

Pavanpati   ("lord of breath") God.

pir   a Muslim spiritual guide or saint.

Pitambar   ("clad in yellow") an epithet for Krishna.

Prabhu   ("lord") one of Krishna's titles.

Prahlada   ("joyous") the ascetic son of Harnakhasa, in whose defence Vishnu took on his incarnation as the man-lion. Prahlada chose to worship Vishnu and performed great penances to acquire the god's favor. His fervor for Vishnu angered his father, Harnakhasa, who tied him to a pillar, drew out his sword, and cried, "Where now is this god of yours?" At once Vishnu emerged from the pillar in his *narsinha* (half-man, half-lion) incarnation and tore Harnakhasa apart, thus saving the son, his devotee, Prahlada. This myth is often used as a parable of God's protection of those who believe in him.

Purana	("old") Hindu holy books that recount the works and powers of various gods. In all, there are eighteen Puranas.
Purukh	("being") a designation for God.
Purushotama	("best of beings") one of Vishnu's titles.
qazi	a Muslim religious judge or magistrate.
Raghunath	("master of the Raghus") an epithet for Rama Chandra, Vishnu's seventh incarnation, and hero of the epic *Ramayana*. In Kabir's songs it is another name for God. Raghu ("swift-one") was Rama's ancestor.
Raghupati	("lord of the Raghus") Rama; for Kabir, God.
Raghurai	("king of the Raghus") Rama. God in Kabir's songs.
Rahman	("compassionate") a Muslim appellation for God.
rai	("king") God.
Raja	("king") God. Also used for earthly rulers.
Rajashram	("high king") God.
Ram	("beautiful," "charming") an epithet for God; not to be confused with Rama Chandra.
Ramananda	a fourteenth century religious reformer; said to be Kabir's guru.
Ravana	("shrieking") the demon king of Lanka, who carried off Sita ("furrow"), the wife of Rama Chandra. This led to the campaign to rescue her, detailed in the *Ramayana*. Ravana was slain by Rama in the final encounter.
Rishi	("seer") a sage or poet, divinely inspired.

Sadhu   ("good," "accomplished") a sage or hermit. This word can also be used as an appellation for God.

sain (swami)   ("lord") a common designation for Brahmins. It is often used in reference to God.

sakhi   a traditional literary figure in Indian poetry, as the confidante of a noble lady in love who confesses her innermost feelings and asks for her advice.

Sanaka   ("ancient") the first of Brahma's four sons who sprang from his mind. Cf. the birth of Athena. All of them chose celibacy and garnered purity.

Sanandana   ("happy") Brahma's second mind-born son.

Sanatana   ("everlasting") Brahma's third mind-born son.

Sanat Kumara   ("ever youthful") Brahma's fourth mind-born son.

Sanda   a semi-divine descendent of Brahma.

sandhya   ("twilight") Hindu prayers recited at sundown.

sangam   ("coming together") the confluence of two rivers, considered holy by Hindus.

Sanjhi   ("friend") another name for the goddess of small-pox (see Hoi).

sanyasi   wandering ascetic.

Sarangdhar   ("bearer of Sarang") Shiva. His bow's name is Sarang ("bow").

Sarangpani   ("holder of Sarang") Shiva.

Shabdi   ascetics who follow the teachings of Gosain Datta. Their full name is "Ekshabdi" ("they who speak

only one word"); and that word is *"Alekh"* ("unin-
scribable," an epithet for God).

Shaivites   the devotees of Shiva.

Shakti   ("power") the creative energy of a god, personified
                  as his wife.

Shankara   ("bestower of peace") a name for Shiva.

Sharda   the goddess Sarasvati, wife of Brahma and patron
                  of Wisdom and Science.

Shastras   the six Hindu philosophical systems, each of which
                  leads to salvation. They are *Nyaya Shastra*, which is
                  concerned with logic and epistemology; *Vaishesh-
                  ika Shastra*, which deals with physics; *Sankhya
                  Shashtra* teaches that being consists of twenty-five
                  basic principles; *Yoga Shastra* embodies religious
                  exercises and acts of self-denial. *Mimansa Shastra*
                  expounds the four Vedas (see Glossary); and *Ve-
                  danta Shastra*, the most important, is concerned
                  with mystical thought. It teaches that the universe,
                  including the gods, is unreal; only the Supreme
                  World Soul is ultimate reality.

Sheshnaga   ("remaining cobra") the thousand-headed serpent
                  that surrounds and supports the earth. It was
                  Vishnu's couch and umbrella when he slept during
                  the cycles of creation carried out by Brahma. It
                  alone remained unchanged while all other matter
                  was reshaped, hence its name. It is also known as
                  Ananta ("endless"). Cf. the Norse world-serpent,
                  Jormungandar.

Shiva   ("auspicious") god of cosmic creation and destruc-
                  tion, the third member of the Hindu trinity.

siddha   ("attained") a very holy and pure sage who has gained semi-divine status and dwells in the regions of the sky, between the sun and the earth. They number 88,000.

Sirjanhar   ("creator") God.

sloka   ("strophe") an octo-syllabic verse, usually two or four lines long.

Smriti   ("remembered") Hindu compendia of traditional law and ceremony. There are twenty-seven in all.

sradha   funeral feast and gifts for ancestors. These are given to Brahmins in the belief that they will reach departed family members. The ceremony also includes offerings of food to dogs, ravens, and other creatures.

Sudama   a childhood friend of Krishna. Since he was extremely poor, his wife suggested to him that he go to Krishna, who was now king of Dwarika. He did so, taking with him a meagre offering of rice. Krishna received him with great respect, and changed Sudama's humble cottage into a great palace.

Sudras   the lowest of the four Indian castes.

Sukhdeva   ("bright god") a sage of antiquity and the son of
(Shukdeva)   Vyasa, the author of the *Mahabharata* and the compiler of the Vedas. Sukdeva became the disciple of Raja Janaka, the father-in-law of Rama Chandra.

Sumeru   See Meru.

Sunya   ("empty") the great void, where the attributeless God lives. To merge into emptiness is the soul's ultimate quest.

Surpati	("lord of the gods") an epithet for Indra, who was king of all the gods.
suttee (sati)	("the true one") a widow who immolates herself on her husband's pyre.
tapi	ascetic.
tilak	ceremonial mark placed on the forehead as a sign of blessing or good luck.
Thakur	("master") God. More specifically, the word means the idol housed in a temple.
Three Worlds (Triloka, Tinloka)	earth, heaven, and middle air (the space between), i.e., all of creation.
Trilochan	("three-eyed," i.e., "seeing into the past, the present, and the future" — an epithet for Shiva) a *bhakti*-poet of the 13th century A.D., who lived near Bombay and was a contemporary of Namdev.
Vairagi	a wondering ascetic who has abandoned the world.
Vaishnava	a devotee of Vishnu and his incarnations.
Vamana	("dwarf") the fifth of Vishnu's incarnations. Bali, a demon, acquired great spiritual power through rigorous asceticism and began to threaten even the gods. In order to defeat him, Vishnu took on the shape of a dwarf and came to Bali and asked for a favor: that he be given as much land as he could cover in three strides. Bali agreed to Vishnu's proposal; at once the dwarf became a giant who covered the earth in the first stride, reached heaven in the second, and with his third touched the middle air in between. As a result, only the infernal regions were left for Bali; Vishnu rescued the rest.

Vedas   ("knowledge") the foundational scriptures of Hinduism. There are four in all: the *Rig Veda, Yajur Veda, Atharva Veda,* and *Sam Veda.*

Vidura   a poor, low-caste man with whom Krishna stayed when he went to visit Duryodhana.

Vishnu   ("pervader") the second member of the Hindu trinity, who sustains all creation.

Vyasa   ("compiler") the sage who, according to tradition, compiled the four Vedas and composed the *Mahabharata.*

Yama   ("strangler," "twin") the god of the dead, who leads souls off in a noose. Cf. Pluto.

Yogi   ("one who yokes") an ascetic who is accomplished in the discipline of yoga. The word "yoga" is etymologically related to "yoke" and can be translated as "spiritual training." This training consists of eight stages, namely *yama* ("self-control"), *niyama* ("paying attention"), *asana* ("posture," the most famous of which is the "lotus-position"), *pranayama* ("breath control"), *pratyahara* ("restraining the senses"), *dharana* ("steadying the mind"), *dhyana* ("meditation"), and *Samadhi* ("intense meditation").

There are four types of yogas. *Raja yoga,* ("royal yoga") which deals with the mind and psychic and intellectual abilities; *Mantra Yoga* ("Yoga of Spells") is concerned exclusively with magic; *Laya Yoga* ("Yoga of Dissolution") involves trances and subconscious processes; the fourth is *Hatha* or *Kundalini Yoga* ("Yoga of Force" or "Yoga of the Serpent") and is largely physical and stresses the *pranayama* stage.

Yoga is broadly a system of salvation. The body has a vein called *sushumna* which runs through the spine, along which are found six circles (*cakra*) of psychic power. At the top of this vein, in the skull, is *sahasrara,* the most powerful psychic centre, commonly called the "lotus." The lowest *cakra* houses the *kundalini* ("serpent power"), which lies inert. Yoga awakens the *kundalini,* and the power rises through the vein, passing through all the six *cakras,* until it joins with the *sahasrara.* This union gives the *yogi* great spiritual power and salvation — the *yogi* is freed from the world.

Index